DRC

SOCIETYNOW

SocietyNow: short, informed books, explaining why our world is the way it is, now.

The SocietyNow series provides readers with a definitive snapshot of the events, phenomena and issues that are defining our 21st century world. Written leading experts in their fields, and publishing as each subject is being contemplated across the globe, titles in the series offer a thoughtful, concise and rapid response to the major political and economic events and social and cultural trends of our time.

SocietyNow makes the best of academic expertise accessible to a wider audience, to help readers untangle the complexities of each topic and make sense of our world the way it is, now.

Poverty in Britain: Causes, Consequences and Myths
Tracy Shildrick

The Trump Phenomenon: How the Politics of Populism Won in 2016
Peter Kivisto

Becoming Digital: Towards a Post-Internet Society
Vincent Mosco

Understanding Brexit: Why Britain Voted to Leave the European Union
Graham Taylor

Selfies: Why We Love (and Hate) Them
Katrin Tiidenberg

Internet Celebrity: Understanding Fame Online
Crystal Abidin

Corbynism: A Critical Approach
Matt Bolton

The Smart City in a Digital World
Vincent Mosco

Kardashian Kulture: How Celebrities Changed Life in the 21st Century
Ellis Cashmore

Reality Television: The TV Phenomenon that Changed the World
Ruth A. Deller

Digital Detox: The Politics of Disconnecting
Trine Syvertsen

The Olympic Games: A Critical Approach
Helen Jefferson Lenskyj

DRONES

The Brilliant, the Bad and the Beautiful

ANDY MIAH
University of Salford, UK

United Kingdom – North America – Japan – India
Malaysia – China

Emerald Publishing Limited
Howard House, Wagon Lane, Bingley BD16 1WA, UK

First edition 2020

Reprints and permissions service
Contact: permissions@emeraldinsight.com

British Library Cataloguing in Publication Data
A catalogue record for this book is available from the British
Library

ISBN: 978-1-83867-988-0 (Print)
ISBN: 978-1-83867-985-9 (Online)
ISBN: 978-1-83867-987-3 (Epub)

ISOQAR certified
Management System,
awarded to Emerald
for adherence to
Environmental
standard
ISO 14001:2004.

Certificate Number 1985
ISO 14001

INVESTOR IN PEOPLE

To Ethan, aim high.

CONTENTS

Preface   vii

Acknowledgements   xv

1. Origins   1

2. Regulating Drones   37

3. The Brilliant   65

4. The Bad   89

5. The Beautiful   111

Conclusion: Drones for Good?   135

References   153

Index   173

PREFACE

The inspiration for this book began in the Autumn of 2013, with a dialogue between myself, the experimental arts festival Abandon Normal Devices and the artist technology collective, Marshmallow Laser Feast. Together, we received funding from the UK's National Endowment for Science, Technology and the Arts (NESTA) to explore the creative potential of drones.

The Nesta fund was interested in how digital R&D could be useful for arts organisations, either in designing products, making production efficiencies or creating new insights that could establish new forms of creative practice. Even beginning the project we were not sure which of these we would fulfil, but there was a strong desire to discover insights that could help arts producers figure out how to use drones within their programmes to create new, different and rich audience experiences.

In one of our first meetings, the title *Project Daedalus* came about, after a discussion about the myth of Icarus. In the context of drones, the story of Icarus was particularly prescient, as drones were, then, still highly experimental devices. We were conscious of the risks associated with flying objects in a modern society, both in terms of safety and in terms of the fragility of the technology, which might easily fail at the crucial point of production. We were also conscious of what Icarus has come to symbolise about the act of flight itself, symbolic of humanity's excessive hubris amid a failure to appreciate the catastrophic consequences that often follow from excessive ambition. As such, we sought refuge in Icarus' father, Daedalus, to characterise the project's values. Daedalus was a craft maker, an artist even, and the creator of Icarus' wings. This was a suitable metaphor for the project, as our goal was to enable flight-based art experiences within the art sector. Yet, we were also informed by Daedalus' cautioning of his son, who told Icarus not to fly too high.

These tethered ambitions were an important operating premise for the project, but we needed to ensure that what we ended up with was much more effective at preventing injury or failure in art productions, than Daedalus was in influencing his son. We wanted to ascertain how we could give practical advice to artists and producers, while also ensuring that we were able to explore the creative limits of the technology. We also wanted to scrutinise the audience experience of such work – without falling into the typical technofetishism that often surrounds innovation. The project would be deeply embedded in the latest technological apparatus and yet we all wanted to interrogate this, question the conventional audiences and consumers of technology and challenge the typical narratives that surround such use. In this respect, the intellectual framework for our research and development was born out of a desire to strip away the technology and focus on the way in which narrative may operate differently through drones – how could they be used for new kinds of storytelling experience?

In the summer of 2014, I took a one-day drone flight course run by Andy Goodwin at Liverpool John Moores University and purchased a couple of micro-drones to practice flying, learn more about the capacity of drones to fly in a semi-autonomous manner, and get to grips with the regulations that surrounded such use. As the project started in October 2014, we were already beginning to see a tidal wave of drone designs and stories emerge in the press. It seemed like not a week went by when there was not a new Kickstarter being launched, or a new headline related to drones. For both the UK and the USA, their principal regulatory authorities – the Civil Aviation Authority and the Federal Aviation Administration, respectively – were each in the process of discussing how best to regulate drones in civilian contexts, which expanded the intellectual frame around the project considerably.

Suddenly, drones were going mainstream and attracting considerable controversy. These developments expanded my interest in drones beyond the project, particularly since it quickly became apparent that producing drone art involved engaging a whole range of issues outside of the practice itself. There were uncertainties about what people could do legally with drones in society, or even what an arts organisation would have to do to ensure that a drone art production was made safe. There were also questions around the security of drones, the cultural meanings they have, the growing ease with which users could operate them and the manner in which their function was also changing, opening out their use to new kinds of demographic.

Something happened to the drone market in late 2014, which led to 2015 being written about as the year of the drone – at least, in terms of consumer technology – justified in part by the proliferation of highly powerful consumer platforms which gave birth to drone communities all over the world. Soon after, such organisations as the Society of Drone Journalists, the World Drone Convention and the New York City Drone Film Festival were established, along with major institutions with governance responsibilities that were trying to figure out society's response to the widespread proliferation of drones.

These happenings influenced how we thought about the utility of Project Daedalus. We had committed to coming up with a tool kit for drone artists, but how could a tool kit be useful in a context where there is constant change taking place and where the volume of money invested in the industry's technological ecosystem far exceeded the project's resources? Over the following months, we became engaged with drone stakeholders across a range of sectors and began to set out a vision for what we needed to consider when thinking about how to get the most out of drones. By then, drones had become a topic of widespread public debate, in part due to the growing consumer market, and the expansion of ways in which drones could be used by civilians for filmmaking or scanning environments.

Central to our work was the collaboration between researchers, technologists and artists, which was the foundation for our inquiry. New modes of discovery are possible by embracing a range of disciplines to ask questions about a single subject. Across our project, the pursuit of producing drone art led us into conversations with the Civil Aviation Authority, Liberty UK, Drone Hackers, Drone Racers, the world of international sports media and much more. This book endeavours to do justice to this period of intense research and development around drone technology but it expands well beyond these years. It addresses some of the key questions we had about how drones could be utilised and the issues that the typical hobbyist might have about how to use them, what they can do and what's around the corner for the industry.

The central thread running through the book is the proposition that drones undertake acts of moral, social, and cultural significance, whether these are for good or bad, and the inquiry proceeds principally to explore this territory. In doing so, I ask questions about where drones are taking humanity and what it may be like to live in a world where there is, for instance, a drone highway in the sky, or drone police patrols, instead of ground constabulary.

In this respect, the book contributes to philosophical inquiries into technology, particularly where there are pressing societal needs to identify the moral import of such devices. In doing so, I am careful not to setup a false dichotomy between drones that one may describe as either unequivocally good or bad, since it is apparent that the goodness or badness of any particular application of technology is highly dependent on its context. For instance, a drone system designed to enhance civilian policing may also jeopardise the enjoyment of individual liberties. Alternatively, such applications may be directly derived from the same drone innovations that are used to undertake military interventions. As such, even where there may be societal value in the transfer of technology from one context to another, its worth may be tainted by the fact that it was designed for some other, more troubling use. Drone weapons may also further complicate the morality of conflict, for instance, by removing the combatant from the field of conflict. Here again, moral tensions exist, as one might also argue that such removal attends to a government's responsibility to minimise the potential for harm that its military personnel may encounter from engaging in conflicts, as Strawser (2010) argues.

It is for this reason that the book discusses the 'the brilliant, the bad and the beautiful' – itself a direct reference to Bijker's (1995) *On Bikes, Bakelike and Bulbs* – rather than set up absolute moral distinctions between contexts of application that are either good or bad. In the same way that Bijker's social history of technology clarifies how the world has been changed by such inventions, this book examines the moral implications of drone technologies while acknowledging that these evaluations are continual subject to re-interpretation. Like biology, technology evolves and adapts in new circumstances where different moral judgements may arise.

Analysing matters of design, development and application, the *first chapter* explains how drones have expanded as a vast consumer market in a very short space of time to become one of the defining technologies of the twenty-first century. It tells the story of the drone's emergence as an object of popular desire and how this reflects a certain kind of technotopian allure, which is found more widely in technological consumer culture.

Chapter 2 considers regulatory concerns around drone applications, discussing the greatest risks associated with their widespread use in civilian airspace. It also examines the development of regulations as evidence of an emerging moral pre-occupation with autonomous machines.

Chapter 3 examines the proposition that drone technologies are a force for good and explores a number of applications that have become prominent within this category. It investigates how drones are being used within a growing number of scientific research programmes and even in such pursuits as journalism to help us better understand the world around us. It focusses on what resides behind the desire to re-characterise drones as objects of desire – and products more generally – and as vehicles for positive social change.

In contrast, *Chapter 4* explores ways in which drones are used for morally contentious applications, while also scrutinising what it is about such uses that is uniquely troubling because they are drones. While our times are characterised by a surge of enthusiasm for the value of drones, so much of the innovation behind their development is achieved because of these destructive ambitions, and for many people, a drone's capacity to undermine human agency through destruction is the most salient anxiety that surrounds their use.

Chapter 5 examines the territory that fits into the realm of aesthetics – neither morally good nor bad, but a new kind of aesthetic sensibility. Framing the conversation around creative applications which encourage us to reflect on our place in the world, this chapter examines the culture of creative drone innovation and artistic practice. In doing so, it considers how drones have been used in performance, spectacle and theatre.

In concluding, the book identifies the direction of travel for the civilian use of drones, providing a glimpse into some novel applications, trends in consumer interest, developments in new designs and questions that remain unanswered about how drones are regulated in society.

Throughout the book, I refer to a range of cultural texts, which speak to the symbolic connotations of drones, as entities that articulate the aspirations and anxieties of many science fiction writers and filmmakers over the twentieth century. Together, these hybrid narratives reveal why drones are so controversial, but also why they are so compelling, as they tell stories of humanity's future and invite us to consider how, like biology, technology also evolves. Moreover, I explore how humanity's conflicting emotions about these prospects is part of a wider technological anxiety that persists about flying robots and the growing incomprehension of artificially intelligent machines, which we are told may have their own volitions.

In closing, the book establishes that drones are morally significant machines, which are creating a culture of acceptance for artificially intelligent automation. There are few technologies which singularly define a period of time and even fewer which resonate with strong anxieties about technological change, but drones are among such examples. Over the last two decades, I have been intrigued by moments of technological discontinuity, an interest that was sparked by reading Ellul's (1964) *Technological Society* and later, Bijker's (1995) work, and this book seeks to attend to the drone's contribution to this trajectory.

My own inquiries into technology have often led me to consider the growing proximity of biological and digital technologies, addressing how our comprehension of the human subject is disrupted by the integration of such technologies within our lives, an interest that persists across this book. Yet, drones are in a category of their own, in terms of what they symbolise about technology's future. Their otherworldliness generates deep anxieties about the age of the autonomous machine and what it might mean for humanity to usher in this new relationship with artifice.

Throughout, the book's focus is on drones that fly, but even this is a subset of the entire range of drones that exist. Today, drone designs encompass moving objects that can operate in the air, underwater and on land, even encompassing all three, or a combination of at least two. While there may be especially interesting discussions to be had within this wider range of vehicles, the focus on flying drones speaks to the mass popularisation of the drone industry. It is these kinds of drones that have created the mass interest in drone technology and which describe most of the consumer market. Nevertheless, there are remarkable drones available that mimic the swimming motion of marine life, in a similar way to how some drones mimic avian flight biomechanics. Such vehicles have huge potential to allow us to explore the hidden depths of the ocean, but it is the flying objects that are most fascinating from a societal and cultural perspective, at least, for now.

ACKNOWLEDGEMENTS

Many people have been crucial to the realisation of this book, mostly through having given time to talk with me about the development of drones. Thanks especially to Gabrielle Jenks for kickstarting my collaboration with Abandon Normal Devices and Marshmallow Laser Feast, where the research behind this project began. Conversations with Robin McNicholas, Barney Steel, Seb Hagemeister, Ersinhan Ersin and Nell Whitley were all pivotal in providing the space to think about the implications of drones. Our funding from Nesta's Digital R&D for the Arts, supported by the Arts and Humanities Research Council, Arts Council England, and Nesta, was a crucial infrastructure for thinking more critically about the relationship between research, art practice and technology.

As well, I am grateful to the many conversations I have had about drones with Serge Wich, Liam Young, Gerry Corbett, Andy Goodwin, Ruth McCullough and Anna Frew. Thanks also to the various organisations who gave me space to speak about this subject over the years, notably BlueDot Festival, British Film Institute, British Science Festival, Cheltenham Science Festival, Institute of Ideas, Manchester Science Festival, Royal College of Art, SciFoo, TEDx Warwick, Manchester Airport, Sheffield Documentary Festival and Sport Accord. Much of the research and the ideas within these chapters began and was developed through giving these talks.

Finally, I am always, particularly grateful to my colleagues and students at the University of Salford, Manchester, UK. The freedom to think across subjects, disciplines, and sectors, bringing industry and academic expertise together in considering questions about our future is critical to all of my work and Salford is a place that celebrates all of these values. Particular thanks to Sheila Pankhurst, Robert Young, Jean Boubli, Judith Smith and our creative technicians at Media City, overseen by Jan Bradley and Tamsin Middleton, who have made it possible for me to share my research into drones with the public since its inception.

1

ORIGINS

Given the volume of debate about drones over the last decade, it is tempting to believe that they are a twenty-first century phenomenon. However, their origins can be traced back to the late nineteenth century and the beginnings of the aviation industry, when pilotless balloons were used in military operations. At that time, the word drone was not used to describe anything resembling the drones that we see all over the world today. Yet, the historical roots of the term drone tell a number of stories that have an impact on how we make sense of the drone today. Its etymology derives principally from an environmental context, where the word drone describes a male bee whose sole function is to impregnate the queen bee. Indeed, the association between bees and mechanical drones designed for military missions is found in the naming of the British remote-controlled plane, called the Queen Bee, which was used in anti-aircraft gunnery training in the 1930s.

First flown in 1935, the Queen Bee had a range of 483 metres, a maximum speed of 167 kilometres per hour and a wingspan of 8.94 metres. It was so successful that the US military subsequently emulated the design, referring to their own plane as a *drone*, in homage to the British plane. This reference conveyed the sentiment that, not only were all the US planes symbolically under the influence of the original Queen Bee, but they were also unmanned aerial vehicles (UAV) requiring a controller to determine their behaviours (Callaghan, 2014; Hilton, 2018; Zimmer, 2013). This early reference to flying insects has led drones to be characterised by actions that are determined by other forces, a kind of mindlessness where its movements are prescribed by a higher authority, which takes decisions on its behalf. In this respect, the drone is devoid of any intelligence or self-determination and functions as a surrogate for humanity's presence in circumstances where people would prefer not to go.

Yet, the origins of the word drone are also found in a completely different and unrelated cultural context: musical composition, where drone music is characterised by a kind of repetitive and systemic sound, a reaction to what Dennis (1974) describes as a 'fragmentation of post-war serial music'. Such music is typified by the work of La Monte Young in the 1960s and later John Cale and the Velvet Underground.

These two completely separate origins were unified in 2014, when pioneering drone filmmaker Liam Young and drone musical pioneer John Cale created a performance at the London Barbican titled *TLoop ≫ 60Hz: Transmissions from the Drone Orchestra* (Cale & Young, 2014), during which Young piloted his drones as integral parts of Cale's musical set (Beaumont, 2014). In this example, we find our starting point for this book, as a way into understanding the contemporary, cultural fascination with drones.

In recent years, drones have attracted widespread discussion with reactions equally amazed and appalled by their exploits. A big part of this tension has to do with the state of our technological culture today and much of this book accounts for the wider technocultural context in which drones exist. The twenty-first century is a time of remarkable technological developments, where automation, artificial intelligence (AI) and the prospects of humanity becoming redundant are intertwined narratives within the cultural discourse about drones. Furthermore, the emergence of new technologies is played out in highly public ways, inviting speculation on humanity's future to a degree never experienced before. Where once, public debate about the future may have been limited to the public square or, later, the professional media, today's public arena consists of billions of messages shared across social networks.

Consequently, drones have become symbolic of a range of societal aspirations and anxieties about technology, a singular technological concept into which diverse aspects of societal interests and functions are located. Other such technological platforms include the mobile phone, the television, the computer, the internet and the automobile. However, the drone is a concept which has unique, diverse properties that speak to a number of crucial dimensions of humanity's ambivalence over its relationship with technology and how it feels about its technological future. Drones are not just single purpose machines. Rather, they are capable of all kinds of actions, from making sports, to making wars and to making film, which is why this book spans the brilliant, the bad and the beautiful. Drones are not just one thing, with a single purpose. They are empty vessels into which humanity may pour all of its desires and all purposes. In this sense, they are radical and revolutionary devices.

In terms of actual flying machines, Hall and Coyne (2014) outline how the development of drones occurred alongside the rise of aviation more broadly and this trajectory remains present today, as drones become a bigger part of military strategies. Indeed, humanity's pursuit of flight is also interwoven with wider ideas about its place in the world. As people have managed to transcend the limits of their evolutionary functions and occupy the skies, so too have they been able to entertain the idea that humans are special and unbound by nature. While these ideas grossly exaggerate humanity's location in Earth's ecosystem, they are views that persist in our society, as humanity's relentless pursuit of discovery reveals.

Drones owe a lot of their popularisation also to contexts which are anything but positive indications of humanity's worth, associated mostly with destruction and surveillance, the use of which scholars have questioned as having only a thin layer of legal legitimacy. In this respect, drones have become championed as technologies of violence and power. In their simplest form, drones allow an operator – or pilot – to occupy the sky in ways that are beyond the capacity of most individuals and, perhaps, through such power, to wreak unprecedented degrees of havoc.

To this end, there is considerable controversy about using the word *drone* within the industry. It is a term that some would prefer to fall out of favour altogether, due to these destructive associations. However, Chapman (2014) provides a thoughtful reflection on the term drone, noting that its popular use is a compelling reason to keep it in play. Chapman (2014) notes further that the

> *push to distance ourselves from the word drone is*
> *primarily coming from one segment of the industry:*
> *the military suppliers and defence contractors who*
> *are now scrambling to move into the commercial*
> *market. (p. iv)*

Yet, to cease using the word drone would be to permit the erosion of this historical reality, which tells the story of the drone industry. Indeed, these relationships also remain a large part of the economic and intellectual infrastructure that surrounds drone innovation today.

Yet, a major shift in public consciousness around drones occurred in December 2013, when Amazon unveiled its plan to radically transform the way it sends out packages to customers, by using drones. At that time, their promotional concept film Amazon *Prime Air* (2015) portrayed a factory in which a drone is loaded with a parcel and is seen flying out to a household. As the film's camera tracks the drone's flight, it then descends onto the pathway of a family's front porch, which they greet happily in anticipation of receiving their goods.

Since then, Amazon has pursued its desire to bring about civilian drone delivery, steadily nurturing the idea that the proliferation of drone services is an inevitable part of humanity's future. Soon after the release of this film, Amazon was accompanied by other commercial giants seeking to do the same. In fact, in April 2019, Amazon was beaten by Google's drone company, Wing Aviation, in conducting the first drone deliveries. A subsidiary of Google's Alphabet Inc parent company, Wing Aviation has been testing drone delivery in Australia since 2014 and is also operating in Finland. Wing Aviation is the first company in the USA to receive a licence to operate as a drone delivery company. Upon receiving its licence, Google explained how:

> *For communities across the country, this presents new opportunities. Goods like medicine or food can now be delivered faster by drone, giving families, shift workers, and other busy consumers more time to do the things that matter. Air delivery also provides greater autonomy to those who need assistance with mobility. Also, our all-electric drones will reduce traffic on our roads and pollution and carbon emissions in our skies. (Wing Aviation, 2019)*

In its Wing Aviation website, it outlines the proposition to customers:

> *What would you like delivered by Wing to your door in less than 10 minutes?*
>
> - *Over-the-counter medicine (such as painkillers)*
> - *Breakfast – I'm in a rush to get to work*
> - *Groceries (toothpaste, washing powder etc.)*
> - *Lunch – I'm too busy at work to grab a bite to eat*
> - *Dinner – there's nothing in my fridge*
> - *'Emergency' essentials (such as diapers, an ice scraper for frozen car windows).*

One of the values of drone delivery systems is that they permit people to send out parcels to any location, whether or not they have a recognised address. Using global positioning system (GPS) data, the package can be programmed to fly just about anywhere, provided the drone has enough battery power to return back to base. The implications of such systems are vast. Societies need no longer be organised around such ideas as a physical address and, much like a phone, the user becomes the node in the network, the point of delivery, characterised by a hidden numerical code, rather than a semantic reference point. Thus, the realisation of drone delivery is a further erosion of our sense of identity and its being replaced by a set of binary codes. In the drone-fuelled future, our locations need not be described by street names, cities or postcodes. Instead, we will have a continually updating GPS location to describe where we are, and all the important places in our lives, transforming how we think of places and the spaces we occupy.

The expansion of drone applications into civilian environments is inextricable from the growth of commercial consumer drone companies, notably Da-Jiang Innovation Technology Co (DJI) and Parrot, two of the leading commercial drone retailers. Their products have become available across a range of retail outlets, which have positioned drones into mainstream conversations. A good example of this is the Apple store, itself a brand which has captured the imagination of digital consumers, not least because mobile phones are quickly becoming control platforms for drones.

As consumer drone use became tied to photography and filmmaking, Apple's alignment spoke to their wider pursuit of what has become known as the prosumer market – where consumers want products that allow them to produce media content of their own, like videos and photographs (Hughes, 2016), rather than simply consume the content of others. In this way, consumer drones emerged as a component of our increasingly digital lives, where everything we do interfaces with our mobile devices in some way. Drones became a crucial lifestyle accessory of that mobile ecosystem.

These examples indicate how the public discourse on drones is changing along with the economic investments around it. A critical part of this history is the various economies and political lobbying that surrounds the development of the drone infrastructure. For example, in August 2015, Amazon created attention by lobbying for drones to be given exclusive access to the altitude of 200–400 feet. This plan conjured up images that are found in countless science fiction stories, where a certain level of the sky above our heads functions as a parallel road network. Since then, Amazon undertook its first drone delivery test flights on 7 December 2016 and has now, like Google, undertaken extensive testing of its delivery system.

These trajectories take the world one step closer to a future of flying vehicles which ferry people around; a prospect that is especially appealing, as the world's roads become ever more congested. However, the means by which this dual layer of vehicular transportation would be powered is still unclear. Moreover, the idea of an additional layer of movement above our heads is not new. Indeed, twentieth century monorails were one such system and subways are a similar concept, albeit underground. What would distinguish a drone highway is the absence of people from the space, but it would still rely on a rule bound, semi-autonomous form of organisation, so as not to create complete chaos.

These possibilities draw humanity even closer to a world that has been imagined by science fiction writers and filmmakers for decades, where, a future of flying machines and artificially intelligent robots would walk – or fly – among us. Indeed, in 1997, the second *Back to the Future* film takes its protagonist Marty McFly to the year 2015, a world where his archenemy has become omnipotent and where hoverboards and flying cars are just another part of the landscape. In this world, these extraordinary technologies have become mundane in the way that describes the trajectory of many mainstreamed technologies, which may be a critical part of their becoming a ubiquitous and seamless part of our everyday lives. At one point in that imagined future, the movie takes us to suburban America to witness how this radical future will affect the lives of the common people. For a fleeting second, we see a flying robot, a drone, taking a dog for a walk. In the future imagined within this film, we are shown how we will send our beloved pets out for walk with robots, rather than take them ourselves. And there may be good reasons to believe this scenario.

Twenty years later, not only did the year 2015 actually deliver the world's first hoverboard, but it has also shown the world's dog-walking drone. In 2014, a film released on Vimeo by Jeff Myers shows a dog waking from its sleep and then being led by a drone around a quiet suburban street in broad daylight, as if it is the most normal thing in the world. While amusing and radical as a proposition, the film's light-hearted narrative frames one of the central questions arising from technology: does it improve our lives? Would people actually seek to send their dogs out with a drone, rather than walk them themselves? If so, then what is it that we value about our lives, or at least, our desire to care for animals? What else would we rather be doing and why would we even have a dog as a pet, if we have no desire to walk with it? The film shows us that, if we so desire, then drones could now do this for us. It presents us with a new way of imagining our lives and many of these ideas are beginning to become a reality.

Three years after Myer's film was released, the online drone sales company 'Drones Direct' was advertising a drone dog-walking solutions on its website. Initially, it showed a DJI Phantom 4 drone attached to a dog via a leash, but, following a letter from DJI condemning the application, it switched to a ProFlight drone. While likely to be a marketing stunt, it shows how ideas in drone fictions shift to drone facts (Charlton, 2017).

The depiction of supposedly aspirational lifestyles is a common feature of all advertising – companies endeavour to sell us a life we have yet to enjoy and which we may seek to experience through our consumption of goods or services. Whether it is the latest computer from the 1990s or the newest Apple iPhone, the design aesthetics of next generation technology seek to convince us that the future is a world of additional creative freedoms and opportunities that will enrich our lives. Consider *Jibo*, an assistant robot that was designed to be a family's helpful organiser. Released in 2017, its bubbly personality (if, indeed, personality is the correct term) and capacity to anticipate its family's needs, sets up the future of robotics as intimately connected to people's everyday needs, from taking photos around the house to reminding us of our day's schedule.

The alignment of robotics, AI and drone technology is evidenced in the history of science fiction and the realisation of technology is revealing how many aspects of these predictions came true. Yet, robots like *Jibo* also have shown how we often get it wrong. In 2019, Jibo's life came to an end, as its producer announced it was ceasing to operate its servers. This was met with widespread reporting of the loss its owners were experiencing after having spent time building a relationship with their robot. With an added level of drama, the robot also announced its own demise to its owners, saying:

> *While it's not great news, the servers out there that let me do what I do will be turned off soon …. Once that happens, our interactions with each other are going to be limited. (Jibo, cited in Carman, 2019)*

Like robots, what fascinates us about drones, is how they compel us to consider our place in the world by making aspects of our contribution to life on earth redundant. In part, this is why there are so many dystopian drone stories in science fiction. Drones convey the gradual removal of humanity from the social world and, more broadly, the absence of biological life on earth. Furthermore, they represent biology being usurped by artifice, albeit an artifice that is reliant on harvesting the requisite minerals that play a crucial part in their construction. Drones emulate the kind of agency that humans have presumed to be unique to them and certainly not possible of replication by a computer. They go even further than conventional robots by enjoying freedom to roam in three dimensions. They ascend vertically with ease, a gesture which resembles levitation and they fly in ways that humans can enjoy only through other technological devices. To this end, drones also confirm humanity's inadequacy and ill-preparedness for the next evolutionary leap upwards.

These two films – *Back to the Future 2* and Myer's dog-walking drone video – speak to a number of aspects of what is happening in the world of drone design today. In one respect, the industry has been experiencing a commercial boom since 2013, led by extraordinary developments in technical design and application. A drone that takes a dog for a walk is now a technical possibility, even if nobody has actually tried it. The short video asks us not only to marvel at the possibilities we imagined decades ago, but also to consider what aspects of our lives we would want to be replaced by robots and which aspects we would like to retain, even if they could be undertaken by a robot. After all, dog owners talk at length about the value of their daily walk with their companion species, the way that it nurtures their bond, and how it enables them a chance in their day to exist outside of other impositions. Consequently, even though it is easy to imagine that our busy lives require having to utilise a drone for dog-walking duties, we might also resist this direction of travel, protesting the erosion of the things that give our lives value, even when we struggle to give them the time we would like. In this respect, the potential use of a technology forces humanity to question the way in which its social world is organised and whether it needs changing. After all, these configurations of decisions operate in specific social contexts which usher them into existence. For example, one may only seek to use a drone to take a dog for a walk, because one does not have time, due to work pressures or other responsibilities. If one removes such pressures, then there may no longer be any such desire for a technological solution.

Through these speculative drone propositions, humanity is asked to consider what kind of future with drones is desirable. The dog-walking drone articulates the promise and peril of technology delivering on both fronts. Indeed, the peril of drones has been an integral part of the discourse surrounding them since their utilisation in mostly military contexts, as I will go on to describe in Chapter 3. However, before discussing such applications in detail, it is useful to further consider the history of drone development, especially recent history, as it explains how drone innovation became the mainstream and how it is connected to a wider aspiration of humanity to transcend limits.

DRONE DESIGN

The starting point for examining developments in drone design can be traced back to the science of aerodynamics, aeronautical engineering or even electronics and physics more widely. Some of the earliest aerial vehicles are critically linked to the most contemporary examples of drone applications. For instance, in 1920, Etienne Omnichen invented the Omnichen 2, a crewed, aeroplane size quadcopter, which flew a record of 360 metres (Tatale, Anekar, Phatak, & Sarkale, 2018). This design proposition has now become the most common consumer drone structure with four rotating blades.

If one narrows the lens further to focus simply on those flying objects that are without pilots – taking a more literal definition of a drone – then one may need to go back at least 80 years, where initial designs in balloon technology were exploring the capacity to pilot, uncrewed vehicles. More recently, the concept of drones is found within vehicles used for space exploration, such as the Mars Rovers, which is among the many artefacts humans have sent out on their behalf to explore what is believed to be the final frontier.

One of the less frequently discussed purposes to which drones are being put is in situations where humans would rather not assume the risks associated with being present. In these circumstances, the drone takes on a kind of surrogate agency on humanity's behalf and we assume their achievements for our own. Thus, the Mars Rover is not an entity in and of itself, but is remarkable only as a conduit of humanity's intentions, as an object that evidences the pinnacle of humanity's evolutionary achievements, enabled by its intellectual accomplishments. Such drone heroes are complex signifiers that bleed into our appraisal of the proliferation of the more domestic drone, as they promise – rather like the promotional drone films – the capacity to transcend our limits; taking our sensorial reach into another dimension. Yet, in doing so, they also perpetuate the sense of unimpeded aspirations for what drones – what flight- may allow humanity to achieve. Indeed, this is one of the crucial features of drones as symbols of our capacity to democratise the experience of flight.

The desire to fly may be one of the most alluring aspects of the appeal of drones. Flying drones allow humanity to reconnect with the technology of flight and, even though we are not physically transported by these devices, they allow us to engage with the principles of aviation and the act of piloting in ways that would otherwise never be available to most of us, were it not for their existence. Most of us will never fly a plane, helicopter or balloon and so, these remarkable achievements in humanity's history remain the achievements of other humans. To fly a drone is to experience the intellectual achievements of those pioneering predecessors and to partake in the consequence of this history making. This is not to neglect one other key historical dimension to this subculture, which is found in the exploits of the model flying community. After all, flying remote-controlled vehicles has been a hobbyist practice for some decades and there are large communities of pilots who play with new forms of drones all over the world.

However, there is something different about drone design and the aspirations of the drone community, which has to do with two related characteristics. The first is the autonomous potential of drones. The reduction of piloting skills to pre-programmable flight paths offers a glimpse of fully autonomous flying systems. Indeed, it is no coincidence that the UAE drone prize launched in 2015 required that all submissions were at least semi-autonomous, as incremental achievements in autonomous control are where the main innovation gains commercially may be found in vehicular transportation. Second, the use of first person view (FPV) goggles, which receive a live video feed direct from the drone's on-board camera, enables the vicarious experience of flight, by providing the sensorial experience of being within the pilot seat without having to be there. Together, these aspects of recent drone designs create a compelling, new proposition for flying objects and a glimpse into the future of new kind of democratised robotics. In this respect, the drone also signifies freedom and the capacity to explore the world more fully.

A SYSTEMS APPROACH TO TECHNOLOGY

Given that drones have been around for decades, what is it about recent times that have led to a boom in the adoption of these new technologies? Have there been some specific technological advances that have allowed drones to become more functional as mass adoption devices? Answering this question requires understanding how the economic context of drone development has changed recently. If one looks back over the history of technological change within society, one can observe key points of innovation that have led to significant social, economic and political change. Whether it is the invention of bicycles, bakelite or bulbs (Bijker, 1995), there are times when a new discovery or invention dramatically changes the kinds of things people choose to do, around which new economies and communities are forged.

One of the features of twentieth century technological design is the manner in which inventions must be understood as components within a system. The automobile cannot be understood outside of the development of the modern metropolis, innovation in road surface technology, the creation of the combustion engine or the ability to access and transform fossil fuels. Similarly, drone technology is an amalgamation of various design trajectories, which come together to make possible new applications. A good example is battery capacity, which remains a key, limiting factor in a drone's flight time. Were it not for progress in battery performance, the flight times and payload capacities of many of the drones I discuss here, would be quite ineffective, creating significant limits in their capacity to function.

Thus, it is the amalgamation of specific design achievements that have allowed drones to become the expanding market that they are today. Batteries, control systems, microchips and 3D modelling software, all come together to make the achievements of the modern day drone possible. Another key example is the development of camera technology, where broadcast quality equipment is available and affordable to amateur electronics consumers and where the usability of such cameras makes possible the capture of content that previously was impossible to achieve. The rise of companies such as GoPro are emblematic of the shift towards affordable, high quality, miniature camera technology, along with the wider development of mobile phone cameras, which have nurtured the amateur enthusiast community. Indeed, in May 2015, GoPro announced that it would release a camera-enabled drone in 2016, which was then launched as the *Karma*, only to be discontinued in 2018 (Martin, 2018).

Were it not for these developments – including those designs that may be described as failures commercially – we would not be witnessing the exponential rise of drones that exists today, but it goes even further than this still. One key aspect relates to software design and the growing intelligence of computers.

Consider the 2015 prototype drone developed by the University of Pennsylvania's GRASP Lab, which used a mobile phone as the on-board–controlled unit of an otherwise dumb drone skeleton (Reyes, 2015). In this case, the phone's camera takes repeated pictures of its environment, so as to understand its terrain and make decisions about how best to fly.

This example of a growing intelligent system underpins the logic of earlier designs and the increased capacities of new drones, which are enabled by some level of intelligent system. One of the best examples of this is found in the work of Raffaelo D'Andrea, whose drones have gained worldwide recognition for the manner in which they demonstrate intelligent learning by a drone. For example, D'Andrea's TED talk from 2011 shows a drone in mid-flight learning how to identify a ball coming towards it and, eventually, figuring out how to hit it back to a thrower. This drone athlete demonstrates how a close positioning system can make possible incredibly precise capabilities but, especially, how AI is a key aspect of what makes drones so remarkable. In the years that have followed, D'Andrea's creations prompted Amazon to purchase his Kiva Systems company in 2012 for $775 million (Lubell, 2016). Central to how D'Andrea talks about his drone creations is the principle that experimental research is fundamentally unpredictable and that each of these achievements in engineering exist at a point of neutrality. It is this neutrality, when assessing the value of technology, that explains why a systemic interpretation of its moral status is critical and drones are a good example of this.

THE RAPID RISE OF DRONES

Alongside examining the enabling consequences of technological innovations, one can also study the economic characteristics that operate around drones. This includes looking at the composition of companies that develop drones, their different price points and capacities they offer, and the range of ways in which they enter consumers' lives through various retail outlets. For example, today, it is possible to purchase drones in bricks-and-mortar toy stores, digital technology stores like Apple or through online retailers like Amazon. These various contexts in which one can obtain a drone are relevant to how one then explains their cultural proliferation and this section articulates some of the key catalysts for the rise of drones.

The reason why Apple began stocking Parrot drones alongside other accessories may be explained in part by the fact that the drone is controlled by their device. An iPad or an iPhone can be used as the control system for Parrot's drone, replacing the traditional controllers that were once more prevalent. The mobile device's accelerometer also introduced a novel dimension to the control system, where tilting the tablet or phone would allow the pilot to steer the drone. In more expensive drones, the mobile phone functions as the monitoring screen and attaches to the controller device, allowing the operator to see the drone's perspective from its on-board camera. It also provides other flight-related data, functioning as the remote monitoring device screen.

However, there is a deeper reading one may make of this alignment, which speaks to the kind of technological culture in which we find ourselves today, where drones are an extension of computers, tablets and mobile devices. The Parrot drones are small enough to be accessible to a wide audience, but powerful enough to capture the kind of film or image content that a company like Apple would seek to champion. Moreover, the gesture-based interfaces offer the kind of glimpse into the future of technology that resonates with the kinds of narratives that operate around the next iPhone or laptop, which trade on a similar aesthetic. In this respect, drones are the ultimate mobile devices, since they have the capacity to move autonomously in three dimensions – they are literally mobile – perhaps the end goal of Apple's vision for fully mobile technology.

The emergence of new companies around such innovation, along with the acquisition of other companies, is an indication of innovation leadership and social change. Google's acquisition of such platforms as YouTube in 2006, or Facebook's purchase of Instagram in 2012, are each indicative of how data-driven acquisitions lead inevitably to embracing drone technology. Indeed, both of these companies – at almost exactly the same time – acquired drone manufacturing companies and each of these companies has invested into drones in order to deliver data to people outside of advanced telecommunications infrastructures.

In Google's case, they purchased Titan Aerospace, which developed high-altitude drones – capable of flying up to 65,000 feet for up to three years – that could have potential applications for delivering balloon-based remote internet delivery and high quality image capture for mapping. Two years after the acquisition, Google shut down the company, integrating its intellectual property into its secret R&D 'X' division for further development.

For Facebook, they acquired Ascenta in 2014, a company that was developing solar-powered drones. The Facebook acquisition was part of its wider plans around its Internet.org initiative, which aims to bring free internet to parts of the world that lack digital infrastructure. The drones' component of this plan – and the appeal of Ascenta – was in the ability to use them as vehicles that deliver connectivity, by their ability to stay in the sky for long stretches of time. The creation of its Facebook Aquila drone was the first attempt to realise the project, but it was discontinued in 2018. Since then, reports indicate Facebook is working with the Airbus military drone, the Zephyr, to continue its aspirations (Russell, 2019).

In sum, examining developments around any single technology provides insight into the catalysts behind an emerging consumer market and explains why it is that technology is such a crucial currency today. As such, it can be instructive to examine the technological design development of drones to shed light on how it is developing as a consumer technology. What is it about drone technology that has led to the recent boom in their discussion within society and the rise of a consumer market? How is it that, seemingly, all of a sudden, drones have become a massive new market of consumer culture?

In answering this question, there are four ways in which one can evidence the expansion of the drone market. *The first* is to examine the range of drone-related patent applications that have been granted. The volume of patents around a particular design concept indicates the emerging commercial market that is expected around the technology and, by examining their origins one may gain insight into what designs have been made available and which elements enter the inventive sphere. Furthermore, while they may not describe the entirety of the historical trajectory of any single technology, patent awards encompass features that are common to the wider development of a new industry sector So, while an inventor may not have patented a design that allows a drone to operate under water, it is likely that soon after the public dissemination of this application, another company will seek to emulate the design and protect it. A *second* approach is to examine the growth of companies that are designing drones, in part drawing on data from the patents. *Third*, it is useful to examine the proliferation of *outsider* designs that operate around the core, regulated industry. Such designs are unlikely to have formal patent protections, but they evidence the emergence of novel modifications that, in turn, may enable new capacities that have generated public awareness, debate and interest. *Finally*, it is useful to examine the historical presentation of drones at major technology expos to identify aspects of design that are driving mass adoption. Together, these elements provide different reference points in the history of design – from conception to public presentation – which articulate how drones became a mainstream part of consumer culture.

A PATENT-BASED HISTORY OF DRONE INNOVATION

The emblematic design of the twenty-first century drone is undoubtedly the quadcopter, an 'omni-directional, vertical-life helicopter drone', as its original patent in 1962 describes. Submitted by Edward G. Vanderlip, the quadcopter has become the single most common consumer drone design, manufactured by countless developers and flown by millions of pilots, amateur and professional all over the world. The quadcopter is also the drone of choice for many, new sectors, such as drone racing, research and surveillance. While variations include the octocopter and the hexacopter, they each rely on the principle of using multiple rotor blades to generate stable flight. Since Vanderlip's early work, multi-rotor drone patents have proliferated, especially since 2010 and their designs tell a story about how drone technology has developed. By examining drone patents, we obtain some insight into the future direction of drone applications, while also gaining understanding into the range of organisations that are driving the drone innovation sector.

Carrascosa and Escorsa (2014, November) published a comprehensive overview of the 'drone patent landscape', which goes some way towards articulating the boom in drone designs from 2009 to 2014. Their investigation of the IFI CLAIMS global patent database revealed 7,670 published documents from 1994 to 2014, comprising 4,357 patent

applications, of which over 50% were ma[ ]
companies, with the USA reaching nearly[ ]

pean and worldwide applications exceeding[ ]
Given this range of patents, it is no coincide[ ]
ing civilian commercial company worldwid[ ] ̣ji,
which was valued at over $15 billion in 2018, reflecting 70%
market share (Yang, 2018).

The patents database indicates that, still, aerospace and
defence contractors dominate drone intellectual property,
notably Thales with patents that cover flight management
and communication systems. Indeed, the dominance of these
companies is also evidenced by the volume of money spent on
drones by the military. Hall and Coyne (2014) describe data
that shows the post-9/11 context in the USA led to increased
spending on drones 'from $363 million in 2001 ($4.77 million
in 2013 dollars) to $2.9 billion in 2013' (p. 453), a shift that
was also apparent in the growth of the proportion of military aircraft that were uncrewed, from 5% in 2005 to 33%
in 2012.

One of the explanations for the proliferation of drone
designs is the innovation that took place around drone
components. Thus, Gertler (2012) notes that, 'in the last
10-15 years ... advances in navigation, communications, materials, and other technologies made a variety of current UAS
missions possible' (p. 6). Gertler (2012) also goes on to show
how aircraft manufacturers have steadily acquired unmanned
aircraft systems (UAS) developers to ensure that their companies remain competitive, as the military move increasingly
towards drones:

> *Companies that have lost out in recent aviation
> contracts, such as Boeing and the JSF in 2001, are
> looking towards unmanned bombers and fighters
> as prospects for growth. Were Boeing to design*

manned aircraft in the future, the critical skills needed would still be present, according to this argument. Boeing acquired UAS maker Insitu in 2008.98 Northrop Grumman Corp., as another example, has created a new business unit to aggressively pursue UAS contracts, and acquired Scaled Composites in 2007 in part for UAS design expertise. (p. 28)

The range of applications for drone patents is also broad. From 2013 to 2014, Carrascosa and Escorsa (2014) reveal how these comprise patents for surveillance systems, transport applications, satellites, solar, agriculture and military uses. Of the 4,357 applications, 1,309 patents have been granted and it is particularly revealing to identify what are the unique and exciting new innovations that underpin these designs. Examining recent patents in detail, some key tipping points are evident in what has spurred on the proliferation of drone technology in recent years. For example, in 2015, numerous companies have sought to achieve a complete 'follow me' system, which allows a drone to follow something or someone, using a tracking device and relational geographic positioning. So, when the tracker moves, the drone moves with it.

A patent review by the USA's National Law Review (Rehm, 2017) shows how the years from 2015 to 2017 show dramatic increases in patent applications, with the continued dominance of France (notably Parrot) and China (notably DJI), which have the second and third highest number of applications, below the USA. It also articulates the top organisations who have been submitting drone patents, with Honeywell dominating at (9%), shortly followed by IBM (6%), DJI (5%), the Boeing Company at (5%), Amazon (5%), Parrot (5%) and Google (5%). Despite this dominance,

50% of patents is from a myriad of other companies, demonstrating how widespread is the number of companies working on drone applications. Organisations such as Samsung and even companies like Domino's Pizza is exploring drone applications (Schibanoff, 2018). Indeed, in 2018, it was shown how drone patents by supermarket chain Wallmart was on track to exceed those submitted by Amazon in 2019 (Coulter, 2019) with its own drone delivery proposition.

Major companies like Amazon have also begun to dominate the patent application market for drone technologies, with a reported 64 patents granted as of August 2017 for 'for delivery drones, including patents for aircraft designs, safety and security systems, methods for transferring goods from the air to the ground, and hive-like fulfilment centers' (Michel, 2017, p. 1). Together, these patents reveal Amazon's elaborate plans for making drone delivery a reality, but also how its innovations seek to influence drone technology more widely, covering such areas as safety features and advances in aerial photography.

THE RISE OF CIVILIAN DRONE MANUFACTURERS

While the patenting data shows the historic dominance of military or aerospace drone manufacturers within the civilian market, it also reveals an emerging cluster of civilian manufacturers, which are changing the landscape of drone design and use. As Chapman (2014) notes, there is a 'new wave of dynamic tech innovators' (p. v) which are beginning to occupy the central stage with creative new innovations and imaginative uses within civilian life. As such, taking a closer look at the rise of these providers offers an insight into how the civilian drone market is developing. The patent data also show a number of prominent start-up companies, which are interested in novel applications, such as use within manufacturing, e-commerce, health, and biotechnology.

A closer look at the patent history data also reveals there are key developers that have emerged in the area. First, there is DJI and Parrot, each of which specialise in manufacturing affordable, hobbyist drones. Most of these fit within the sub-7-kilograms range – many can weigh just a few grams and can be purchased in toy stores. The slightly larger size of the DJI's and Parrots are capable of creating professional level film footage using popular consumer products such as GoPro cameras or their own cameras.

Another key emerging demographic for drone developers is children. Although many of the larger consumer drones like Parrot and DJI recommend that only older children fly their drones and certainly with parental supervision, there is no fixed legal obligation to be of a certain age to pilot such drones. For really young people, the smaller drones are designed and marketed as toys. Among these are the Hubsan nano and the Parrot's mini drone range, early versions of which were given fun names like the Spider and Sumo drone. Anything heavier than this and advice varies as to the recommended minimum age for operators. Indeed, public opinion about such rules varies too. In the UK, the Civil Aviation Authority's (CAA, 2016) drone survey found that 69% of the public considered that a minimum age should be established, with the age of 17 identified as the preferred threshold.

This overview of new drone manufacturers provides further insight into the growth of the civilian market. Yet, the resulting attention to this new economic sector does not provide a full insight into what is happening around drone innovation. Omitted from this analysis is a range of new companies and component manufacturers, which are still below the radar in terms of impact, but whose designs are highly influential in drone technology. Indeed, identifying a drone manufacturer is getting more and more challenging, since companies, whose core services and products have not involved drones are finding themselves involved with making them or working on drone applications to amplify their wider provision. A good example of this is the company FLIR, which specialises in thermal imaging and has embarked on collaborations with US-based *DroneSense* (FLIR, 2019) and Chinese drone developer DJI (DJI Technology Inc., 2015). Indeed, one crucial feature of the rise of civilian drone technology is the story of how collaborations have been forged across developers of different drone components to make better artefacts. Drones are a logical next step for camera developers where, presently, the approach is for the user to simply find a way of attaching a camera to the system, or for the developer to use their own camera, which may be inferior to those made by leading producers in camera and lens equipment.

OUTSIDER DESIGNS

While the historical overview of patents and the range of companies involved with designing drones provide one historical overview of this sector, the drone developer community also operates outside of these structures, with a number of users building their own drones from a range of components. While there may be a similar economic footprint to these components – for example, building one's one drone still requires accessing microchips, motors, blades and batteries from suppliers – the range of design applications is yet more varied than is apparent from surveying just the commercial manufacturers. A number of open source drone platforms have proliferated in recent years, including the Paparazzi UAV, ArduPilot and Dronecode, There is even a design called *Flone*, which transforms a mobile phone into a drone (Baker, 2018).

Its designers seek to democratise drone technology, providing a DIY kit to help anyone transform their mobile phone into a drone (Parkinson, 2014).

One of the interesting features of drone technology today is how they compare to other technological devices. It is more common today for consumers to purchase devices that operate within relatively closed systems, within which obsolescence is a design feature rather than an unfortunate consequence of the design. Indeed, the concept of planned or designed obsolescence may be inextricable from a capitalist society, which is reliant on the continual consumption of new services and products.

A more recent characteristic of consumer technology is denying the user the opportunity to repair or maintain their device themselves, forcing them to replace it or utilise the product's maintenance service to enable the continued use of their purchase. Whether it is a new car or a new computer, producers have increasingly designed out the possibility of user maintenance and modification. Cars now rely on inbuilt computer systems to diagnose repair and it has become almost impossible for an owner to undertake maintenance themselves, beyond the most basic interventions. It is explained as an innovation in service culture, but it is also disarming the consumer from asserting any agency beyond simply the act of consumption. In this respect, one of the features of the modern day operating system is its being largely incomprehensible by the average consumer. Drone technologies are novel from a design perspective, because one of their features is to resist such limitations.

While there are now many consumer drones available for purchase that are relatively closed systems, there are more examples of drones that can be modified and even hacked by their users. For example, in 2015, the leading commercial developer DJI launched a developer version of a drone, which would allow this capacity and this design proposition may signify the coming of age of the drone hacker movement. The consequences of this new culture of *prosumption* remain unclear, but it is akin to Apple switching to an open Android operating system and inviting others to design for its platform, rather than building its own. Furthermore, innovation is enabled by what may be analogous to the kinds of user group that surrounds such technologies as Raspberry Pi; the desire to intervene in the creation of computing applications is apparent around the drone user community. It may be easy to provide an open source option, when holding a significant proportion of the market share. Yet, while DJI retains its comparatively closed designs for wider commercial use, the move is a strong shift in the direction of open source drone design, the impetus of which may be the growth of the DIY drone community – and the maker movement more widely – along with the realisation that drones need to have bespoke solutions to perform the range of tasks that people expect from them.

The drone user community is one instance of a wider movement of people who are trying to reclaim control of technological systems, a push back against the alienating consequences of closed, corporate systems, which disempower users and limit the capacity to understand our world. Examples of resistance are found in such technologies as Phonebloks, a project which advocated a completely modular mobile phone. In this case, the organisation aimed to inspire designers to allow owners to swap out old phone components for new, making it a system capable of continual modification and enhancement, as new, better, components become available. Within their documentation, the makers of Phonebloks (2015) explain their belief 'that all our electronics should be built like this, modular. With one universal platform for the whole world'. Jablonowski (2015) describes the DIY drone maker community as a manifestation of the public's desire to reclaim technology as value neutral. Such efforts and frustrations lead someone to create a 'chococopter' – a drone whose frame is made of chocolate – to reinvigorate the technologically disempowered to find their place within the techno-political milieu.

DRONE EXPOS AND THE KICKSTARTER ECONOMY

A final indication of how rapidly consumer drone technology has risen in the last few decades – and what it tells us about the future of drone designs – is discovered by examining how drone developers have positioned themselves within the public's imagination. Drones have become central pieces in a new kind of science fiction consumerism, where customers pre-order their objects from the future, in the hope of occupying the imaginative space their proposals describe within a reasonably fixed timescale. A key component of these journeys is their being showcased at new products at major international expos. Such events have become remarkable storytelling experiences, rather like the International Expos and World Fairs of the 19th Century. This final section examines how drone futures have been imagined in recent years, not by writers of science fiction, but by developers who promise a time-line on the realisation of these potential futures and who employ creative media to sell the public the idea of what drones will be able to do, if only people pay up front.

In doing so, it analyses a number of drone projects from the crowd-funding platform Kickstarter and the world-renowned CES show from Las Vegas from 2011 to 2019. Together, these contexts speak to the developmental chain of consumer products as they approach the market and so speak to the emergence of future experiences of technology. As such, they offer an insight into which manufacturers have led the drone innovation market internationally. More interestingly, they articulate what has been imagined as the aspiration for drone use in the consumer market, giving a sense of what designers consider to be the most interesting opportunities arising from drone technology. The summary data in this section are taken from Google searches of CES and Kickstarter drones projects cross-referenced with search results from their own platforms.

Kickstarter

Since Kickstarter's launch in 2009, it has hosted over 460,000 projects (Szmigiera, 2019) and drones have been among the most ambitious of those. As a cultural phenomenon, Kickstarter reconstitutes consumer culture by asking the public to invest into the concept of a product, before it has been fully developed. Historically, such investments might have been left to professional investment companies or individuals who have, perhaps, large amounts of wealth and use investments as part of their business or income generating strategy. In fact, Kickstarter describes its users as investors and the credibility of any project is wholly reliant on being able to provide a compelling proposition that a customer may deem to have a realistic chance of completion. Kickstarter projects ask customers to buy the product in advance, to support its development. The reward may give the investor early access to the product or a range of additional rewards. The experimental nature of Kickstarter projects means that many of them fail to deliver, though Kickstarter has strict guidelines over what it judges to be a realistic project. Yet, all projects are imbued with a degree of promise that has yet to be realised and a degree of risk. In this sense, a choice to invest money into a Kickstarter project is both a gamble and an investment.

Kickstarter (2019) recognises that its economy is entirely reliant on 'a system of trust' and its terms of use emphasise the importance of transparency and honesty in communicating what a project will deliver. It also emphasises that it does not 'step into the creative process' with projects, which encompasses this process of storytelling about what they promise. This is especially relevant for drones and other technology products, which often rely on visual articulations of what the product will look like eventually. However, projects are subject to wider rules around false advertising, as with any consumer product.

The challenge is that many of the promises made within Kickstarter projects are articulated often only as conceptual propositions, explanations of a proposed working design; where this public presentation must rely on some degree of fabrication, since the product is not yet made. These details are especially relevant to emerging technology projects, since they rely on a kind of storytelling, the ending of which is highly dependent on being able to resolve a number of unpredictable technical challenges. The story told about these projects often relies on the use of creative, promotional films that allude to the product's use, even if it does not show it in use.

In 2019, there were over 60 drone projects listed as investments on Kickstarter, including such projects as Hover 2's 'the 4K drone that flies itself', the Mystic drone that 'sees and understands' permitting gesture-based interactions, and Fleye 'your personal flying robot'. This figure consists of fully developed drone projects from 2011 to 2019, but excludes drone component projects. Among this number, many of them have failed to reach their funding target, their project campaign pages are a graveyard of visions for the future that never captured the public's imagination. Many of these projects reflect the values of the emerging consumer drone market at the time, encompassing such functions as follow-me technology, high end camera capabilities, heightened portability and ease of piloting. By analysing the stories of these campaigns, one learns that drone designers seek to extend the functional ease of the mobile phone era. In so doing, they champion intuitive, unskilled and portable designs that allow people to capture the lives they lead in films and photographs, which are the dominant design functions of the consumer drone. Design features in new projects emphasise such functionality as being fully waterproof, or being completely hands free. Kickstarter also tells the story of the emerging drone racing market and the rise of companion robots, as drones are given such personalities and characteristics that encourage users to think of them as life forms. The 'AirDog' (2014) raising over $1.35 million on Kickstarter will loyally follow its user and even comes with an 'AirLeash' to switch between trackers.

Consumer Electronics Show 2013–2019

The point at which drone propositions become closer to realisation is well articulated by their being shown at international expositions, of which one of the most notable is the Consumer Electronics Show (CES) in Las Vegas, USA. However, this is not always the case. Some products may showcase at CES before launching their Kickstarter campaign, as for the Mystic (2018) drone. In this case, the developers also acknowledge that development continues, despite having a working prototype. On its Kickstarter page, Mystic states 'While the main product development is already completed, our team of skilled technicians is daily adding new features and perfecting the Mystic's performance to ensure that our valued customers receive the best possible autonomous UAV experience' and emphasises, some of the values exhibited within the Kickstarter projects, notably ease of use.

The Mystic (2018) developers state how the drone offers 'the ultimate aerial video and photography experience, creating breathtaking imagery without the need to learn complicated film techniques'. In this sense, CES complements Kickstarter as a creative, innovative space, characterised by products that are approaching the market with some commercial propostion.

Being one of the world's most high-profile technology events, the CES programme brings together companies from all over the world to attract media excitement about their project's completion and has become the 'primary show-case for the drone industry' (Reagan, 2016). Analysing the media coverage of CES for the last decade shows that drones first made appearances from 2010 with Parrot's AR.Drone. Moreover, drone demonstrations have grown at CES ever since, growing significantly in 2016 with an Intel keynote talk heralding a world-record breaking drone choreography. The year 2016 also reveals a landmark in the media cover-age of drones at CES, with feature summary articles from major media outlets. Some reported that drones feature as gimmicky toys designed to attract media attention at CES, rather than being serious technological innovations, which speaks to the fascination around drones (Popper, 2017). In 2017, the FAA even gave a speech at CES talking about the drone 'revolution' and the urgency to ensure rules governing drone operations are reasonable (Huerta, 2017).

One of the key insights from Kickstarter and CES is that, since 2013, the growth of drones has grown significantly, as an artefact of public interest, a metaphor for technological innovation across a number of technology sectors. Together, they also articulate the range of consumer sectors in which drone industries have first developed, such as drone racing, drone research and drone photography/filmmaking. Products like the EHANG 184 passenger drone also show how drones are objects of far-future gazing ideas, mechanisms of imagining a new kind of social reality and this aspect of technology's currency is central to their cultural value. In cases like this, it matters less whether the product will arrive any time soon. Instead, what matters is to showcase the innovative vision for the future. Such products, many of which are never realised, invite the public to consider the future and to invest insight into that future within the company's brand.

A good example of this was found at CES in 2016 when the Lily Camera drone was first presented. Its self-described 'throw and fly' interface was revolutionary, needing nearly no technical flying skills at all. The user could simply throw the drone in the air and it would figure out that it needed to fly. Yet, in January 2017, Lily announced its closing and would return its $34 million investments back to customers, none of whom ever saw the magical Lily drone (Deahl, 2017). Moreover, the day after this announcement, the San Francisco District Attorney filed a civil consumer protection suit alleging the company's launch video was 'false and misleading' in its depiction of what Lily could do (*The People of the State of California* v. *Lily Robotics, Inc.*, 2017). Later that year, Lily re-launched, attempting to honour initial investments, but again subsequently seemed to shut down in 2019 (Murison, 2019).

Another good example of the speculative consumerism that exists around drones is Nixie, a project proposition which was launched in 2014. Described as the world's first wearable drone, Nixie fits around the user's wrist like a watch and will open out into a quadcopter and fly on command. The promotional film from 2014 depicts a climber high up on a rock face who then activates the drone, which flies off and captures stunning film of the climber as she completes her ascent. As with the *Lily* selfie drone, their application is communicated first in a form of pseudo-documentary, giving the viewer an idea of what Nixie will eventually feel like, once available (Fly Nixie, 2014). Nixie's promotional film portrays ideal users, free from the burden of needing to engage with the technical challenge of piloting, free to enjoy the activity they are engaged with.

Five years later, the *Nixie* drone is still generating media coverage, but the product has yet to materalise. The website is no longer available and its Wikipedia entry describes it as in development since 2016. Nixie's Facebook page has not been updated since 2017 and the latest YouTube video is produced at CES in 2016, showing a working prototype which looks very different from the drone design portrayed in its promotional video from 2014 (Engadget, 2016). Yet, the absence of Nixie to materialise is not really relevant to the claims I wish to make about its value. Rather like the Kickstarter projects, products like Nixie ask humanity to consider the lifestyle they might seek to enjoy by having novel products, which promises to give us new perspectives on the world around us. Nixie's project manager, Jelena Jovanovic, describes how the company is 'not trying to build a quadcopter, we're trying to build a personal photographer' (cited in Flaherty, 2014) and this speaks volumes to what technology developers are trying to do today, to remove the need for users to attend to the technological interface. In this sense, the ideal interface is one that requires the least amount of conscious thought from the user.

While there are certainly serious implications to a product failing to deliver, notably ensuring that the investors are reimbursed, there is a broader social value to these projects which has to do with publicly evidencing the innovation process. Their value as speculative projects is greater than their deployment, as their conceptual propositions for what may be desired in the future offers insight into humanity's relationship with technology and what it says about what people value. Yet, as for the *Fleye* drone, the success or failure of products also provides insights into the state of an industry and the degree to which it is capable of allowing small start-up companies to flourish, or if large organisations occupy too much of a monopoly to permit such innovations from materialising.

In both the Kickstarter projects and the CES showcases of drones, we glimpse the future of drone technology. Yet, rather than simply think of them as products to be consumed, these speculative designs should be treated as hybrid cultural texts, new forms of science fiction. The Kickstarter projects are the science fiction stories we all can author by making a financial contribution to their development. They constitute a crucial component in the story of the proliferation of drones in contemporary society and designate a new kind of consumerism that sustains these future economies. The drone with the best story is likely to be the one that wins the most funding, but this does not mean that we will ever see it.

CONCLUSION

In concluding this opening chapter, it is critical to note that the rise of the popular fascination with drone technology is found along a continuum which ranges from moral panic to fascination for the new possibilities that drones bring. Drones promise to push humanity into a radical future where the imaginations of science fiction writers from years gone by become a reality. Organisations like Facebook, Google, Apple, in collaboration with drone manufacturers such as DJI and Parrot, along with the interplatform collaboration that these devices utilise, go some way to explaining why it is that we find ourselves amidst a drone revolution. But, how has society responded to such transformations and have we figured out how to deal with their impacts? The next chapter focusses on the regulatory context surrounding drones, as a way of explaining which principles govern the use of drones and which moral questions they challenge us to address.

2

REGULATING DRONES

One of the key challenges facing the drone user community in recent years has been the dynamic regulatory changes that have been implemented. In fact, while many hobbyist drone pilots may regard their use of drones to be free from restrictions, the rules administered by the aviation authorities around the world already encompasses the operation of drones to some degree and consist of quite tightly controlled conditions in which drones may be flown. As such, anyone who operates a flying vehicle in open air space in many countries – and often indoors too – is wise to learn about their local laws or risk transgression into serious crimes without even realising it.

Yet, only since around 2000 there have been specific guidelines in many countries for drones, as opposed to rules that govern aviation more generally. For example, in the UK, the CAA published an operation guide in 2001, which set out its core principles and guidance for operators and pilots. In 2015, it undertook a complete revision of this guidance (CAA, 2015a), introducing areas of concern that reflect the direction of travel for technological change, such as the rise of intelligent drones. A further edition is published in 2019, modifications of which provide greater restrictions on drones in specific geographic areas of high risk (CAA, 2019).

In 2014 and 2015, the need for clarity on drone operations in civil society was fuelled by the rapid proliferation of consumer drones made available on the high street. Moreover, the professional market has risen considerably over a five-year period. In the UK, there 'are now almost 5,000 permissions for commercial drone operations in the UK, having doubled since February 2017 and increased from just five in 2010' (Haylen, 2019, p. 5). In the USA, since the government implemented a mandatory drone registration scheme in December 2015, there have been over 1 million drones registered, which breaks down as 878,000 hobbyists and '122,000 commercial, public and other drones' (U.S. Department of Transportation, 2018) with an annual growth rate of 'around 13 percent' (FAA, 2019a).

In this context, this chapter outlines some of the key regulatory challenges surrounding drone use in civilian contexts, while also analysing trends within regulation. These details reveal a range of concerns about the direction of travel for drone applications, particularly for uncertificated hobbyists, for whom drones function as potentially dangerous toys used often for leisure filmmaking and photography. Beyond describing present day rules, the chapter also examines the wider moral and safety considerations that pilots must take into account, even if they are not yet enshrined within legislation.

DRONE INCIDENT REPORTING

With the growing use of drones, there has also been an increased number of drone incidents, with the UK's police reporting a change 'from 94 in 2014 to 425 in 2015' (Yeung, 2016) and a rise of airport-related incidents by 30% from 2017 to 2018. While the consequences of these incidents are varied and their significance contested, many of them attract considerable press coverage, perhaps the most infamous of which has been the disruption at Gatwick airport by an unknown drone operator in 2018.

Indeed, in 2019, the BBC produced a documentary titled *Britain's Next Air Disaster? Drones*, which framed the future of drones in terms of the risks they present to create possible disasters that could lead to the loss of human life. The documentary prompted world-leading drone developer DJI to write a letter to the head of the BBC, protesting its sensationalising and misrepresenting the risks. In the letter, DJI's Director of Communications, Prof. Barbara Stelzner (2019) complains of biased reporting, arguing that its overarching militarised undertone created a sense of alarm and imminent danger, which does not describe the majority of drone operations by consumers.

The documentary reveals how the media discourse on drones remains very focussed on telling stories of near disaster, despite the safety standards of drones having vastly improved over the years. In part, this is due to a number of high-profile incidents, which have occurred in different parts of the world, often through reckless flying. In addition to those already mentioned, others include a hobbyist losing control of his drone in the USA during 2015, which saw the drone landing on the lawn of the White House (Greenwood, 2015). This incident prompted drone developer DJI to widen their inbuilt flight restriction zones to their drones, including the downtown D.C. within the revised maps. [1] In fact, since 2014, DJI has designed their drones with inbuilt geographic restrictions to avoid hobbyist pilots from making dangerous errors. These restrictions keep expanding as incidents arise. As Poulsen (2015) reports:

> *The company first added no-fly zones to its*
> *firmware in April of last year to deter newbie*
> *pilots from zipping into the restricted airspace over*
> *airports, where they might interfere with departing*
> *and arriving aircraft. If a Phantom 2 pilot flies*
> *within five miles of a major airport's no fly zone,*
> *the drone's maximum altitude begins to taper. At*
> *1.5 miles away, it lands and refuses to take off*
> *again. Municipal airports are protected by smaller*
> *zones, also programmed into the drones' firmware.*

In 2019, these principles have remained relatively stable for DJI drones, but with additional capacity to approve exceptions within 30 minutes of receiving applications. Moreover, its more sophisticated system provides additional nuances to the no-fly-zone perimeters:

> *The GEO system previously geofenced a 5-mile*
> *circle around airports, with enhanced restrictions in a*
> *smaller circle encompassing the airport area. GEO 2.0*
> *applies the strongest restrictions to a 1.2 kilometer-*
> *(3/4 mile)-wide rectangle around each runway and*
> *the flight paths at either end, where airplanes actually*
> *ascend and descend. Less strict restrictions apply to*
> *an oval area within 6 kilometers (3.7 miles) of each*
> *runway. This bow tie shape opens more areas on the*
> *sides of runways to beneficial drone uses, as well as*
> *low-altitude areas more than 3 kilometers (1.9 miles)*
> *from the end of a runway, while increasing protection*
> *in the locations where traditional aircraft actually fly.*
> *(DJI Technology Inc., 2018b)*

Elsewhere, the Pirate Party flew a drone into a public space where German Chancellor Angela Merkel was giving a speech. The stunt was conceived as a protest against the

German government's use of drones in military contexts, but its main impact was to reinforce how easy it would be for somebody to use a drone for disruptive, criminal, and even terrorist practices in civilian locations (Gallagher, 2013). These events have led to greater demands on the aviation authorities and the creation of new rules to govern the use of drones. They have also led to investments into anti-drone systems in various settings, especially around aerodromes.

Despite questions over the safe proliferation of civilian drones, there are significant pressures from commercial organisations to establish systems and protocols that will permit the full exploitation of drone technology, as described earlier in the case of drone deliveries. In this case, even if drone delivery is not something people use for all of their deliveries, the drone delivery market is growing rapidly, as more people expect instant service from online shopping. Indeed, the range of parcels that could be delivered is expanding well beyond simply consumer goods. For example, in May 2019, for the first time, a human organ was delivered by a drone to a hospital for a surgical transplant. Flying a kidney from the University of Maryland in the USA to University of Maryland Medical Center, the drone covered a distance of nearly 3 miles in just less than 10 minutes and was successfully transplanted to the patient (Dent, 2019). Also, in 2019, Drone Delivery Canada was awarded its first US patent for Flyte, which proposes the creation of a 'railway in the sky' on which various drone providers could plan their flight path across a network of established flight routes (Di Benedetto & Colacitti, 2019).

THE UK AND THE USA RULES

The rules governing drone flights in civilian space focus mostly on safety concerns and the risks associated with drones colliding with people or property. In the USA, there has been caution and uncertainty about how best to legislate for risks associated with drone use. Despite Amazon's persuasive power as a transnational company, the USA's FAA has been reluctant to embrace drone delivery services and a big part of this has to do with the risks associated with flying objects proliferating around air space that is still largely unresolved logistically. Indeed, aside from the self-evident fact that flying objects with rotating blades around people is likely to be risky, there is some precedent for evidencing the dangers. For example, in October 2013, a drone pilot flew their vehicle around Manhattan, eventually crashing into a building and almost injuring a pedestrian below. In a statement to the media, an unnamed NYPD officer said 'We can't have random people flying unmanned aircrafts over New York City' (cited in McNulty, 2013).

While drones bought from an Apple store as a luxury toy with remarkable automation capabilities may appear benign, there are many risks to such use, the most obvious one of which is the pilot's capacity to lose control of the drone. While the technology has improved dramatically in recent years, drones can sometimes lose connection with their controllers, described as a loss of telemetry. Alternatively, drone pilots may not undertake the necessary practice to ensure that they can control their drone in unexpected circumstances. This is especially worrisome when coupled with a culture of high expectations in digital devices. Today, people expect technology to work, without much investment to learn the system. In the case of a mobile phone or a television, the implications of failing to learn the system are quite minor, but for a flying vehicle with rotating blades, they can be life-threatening.

This is why there is now a list of recommendations that surround the use of hobbyist drone operation and also why there is a clear distinction between such use and drone flight for commercial purposes. Most of the drones that one can buy on the high street do not exceed a weight of 1.5 kilograms and the level of risk associated with a drone is reasonably proportional to its weight and size. While a significant amount of damage can be done to an individual with a drone of only a few centimetres in diameter, near fatal injuries can occur with drone of anything greater than 1.5 kilograms.

In this respect, aviation authorities typically distinguish between commercial and hobbyist drone operations, in recognition of the additional level of responsibility that goes along with operating a heavier drone. Indeed, larger drones tend also to be the kind that require heavy attachments mounted on them, such as professional camera equipment. Yet, while historically there were greater requirements for commercial operators to be qualified and register their drones, there are now growing expectations that recreational pilots will be subjected to even greater rules. For instance, in the USA, as of May 2019, the FAA Reauthorization Act came into force, requiring a hobbyist to register as a 'modeler' and ensure that their aircraft is labelled with their registration number (FAA, 2018). Pilots must be at least 13 years old – or, if younger, then someone older must assume legal responsibility. Recreational fliers must also be a US citizen or a 'legal permanent resident', with capacity to register their email address, credit or debit card and physical address.

These rules do not apply to toy drones weighing less than approximately 250 grams and there are further restrictions if the drone weighs over 25 kilograms (FAA, 2019a). Recreational drone users will also be required to prove their competence through test and certification, which will cover a range of the following areas of knowledge:

• Applicable regulations relating to small UAS rating privileges, limitations and flight operation.

- Airspace classification and operating requirements, and flight restrictions affecting small unmanned aircraft operation.

- Aviation weather sources and effects of weather on small unmanned aircraft performance.

- Small unmanned aircraft loading and performance.

- Emergency procedures.

- Crew resource management.

- Radio communication procedures.

- Determining the performance of small unmanned aircraft.

- Physiological effects of drugs and alcohol.

- Aeronautical decision making and judgment.

- Airport operations.

- Maintenance and preflight inspection procedures (Federal Register, 2019).

In the UK, a similar conversation has taken place over the same time span. By 2015, the industry had pushed for greater freedoms for users, but amateur drone users continued to operate in high risk situations, ignoring the CAA's regulations in terms of distance from people and built up areas. Since July 2018, the CAA restricts drone users to an upper altitude of 120 metres. When flying above this height, a pilot must submit a Notice to Airmen (also known as a NOTAM), which alerts other pilots in the area of activity that is taking place. The pilot is also responsible for identifying where there exist no-fly zones within their intended flight path and is legally required to respect these. Additionally, the CAA indicates that no flights are permissible in built up areas, particularly where the general public may be within 50 metres of the flying vehicle, and no flying can occur above the heads of the public, at whatever distance it might be. All of these rules are neatly summed up in the CAA's Drone Code, which states the following:

> *Don't fly near airports or airfields*
>
> *Remember to stay below 400 ft (120 m)*
>
> *Observe your drone at all times – stay 150 ft (50 m) away from people and property*
>
> *Never fly near aircraft*
>
> *Enjoy responsibly.*
>
> (CAA, 2019, July)

Other rules include restrictions on undertaking flight for commercial purposes, which require a professional, recognised qualification, being of a minimum of 16 years old and having appropriate insurance. The flying vehicle must be designated as air worthy – for UAVs in excess of 20 kilograms (CAA, 2015a, p. 90) – which may be assumed for commercially available drones, but for anything bespoke or homemade is not guaranteed.

There are two recent changes to the UK's CAA's guidance that are particularly important. The first is that, from 1 March 2019, the previous 1 kilometre restriction around airports and airfields has now been replaced by the location's specific own airfield perimeter guideline. Additionally, the July 2019 Drone Code indicates that recreational drone pilots will be required to demonstrate competence through taking a drone test online, though this has not yet been formalised and remains open to consultation.

One of the reasons why drones are controversial and why these additional rules are required is that previous guidelines are not being upheld by a growing number of drone pilots who simply purchase their drone in the high street or online and go out to play. Indicative of this is the fact that public parks have had to install no drone flying notices, but still, people continue to fly in dangerous circumstances. Since 2014, high-street stores have sold highly sophisticated drones that are capable of flying at extremely high altitudes and fast speeds. In the UK, one of the key stores to pioneer such sales is the technology shop Maplin. Indeed, in 2014, Maplin attracted criticism over its release of a drone film, which depicted one of their stock DJI quadcopters ascending in a built up area, next to one of its branches. The backlash to this film was intimately connected to the CAA's concerns about public safety and wider regulatory authorities interests to maintain order within society.

In December 2014, Maplin released guidelines for promoting the safe use of drones, which broadly echoed the principal CAA requirements at the time. These guidelines state the following:

1. You are totally responsible for the safe conduct of each flight.

2. You must keep the drone with your sight at all times.

3. You are responsible for avoiding collisions with other people or objects – including aircraft, plan your flights beforehand if necessary.

4. You must keep your drone at least 150 metres away from a congested area (such as residential streets, town centres, etc.).

5. You must not fly your drone within 50 metres of a person, vehicle, building or structure, or over groups of people at any height.

6. If you intend to use your aircraft (with camera) for any kind of paid work you must obtain permission from the CAA.

7. Never fly your aircraft near any airport, airfield or power installation (such as substations and pylons).

THE EROSION OF SKILLED PILOTING

While useful for the new hobbyist, it is hard to support the claim that the enhanced guidance has led to a culture of responsible flying, even if the majority of hobbyist flights take place without any incident. However, the bigger challenge is the culture of unskilled flying that has emerged around sophisticated and powerful consumer drones. Today, to fly a drone, one does not even need to know how to control the device using a standard control interface and this is, in fact, celebrated by drone developers.

Consider the IRIS+drone from 2014. In the promotional materials surrounding its commercial release, the values of this drone were located in its being capable of operation with nearly no skills at all. The pilot could simply draw a flight path along a map on a mobile or tablet and the drone would fly off and complete that route. Such drones were capable of flying semi-autonomously; the pilot could pre-programme the drone's flight path using its software and send it on its way. While this is perfectly adequate in the main part, the problem occurs when the control system fails and the pilot then has no skill set to deal with the eventuality.

Indeed, before sending a drone into the sky, it is sensible for a pilot to have the capacity to deal with an unexpected loss of automated control to ensure that the drone can be landed safely. Yet, there is no such requirement when flying the Iris+and – as such functionality became commonplace in many drone subsequently – to enforce such skills would require a nationwide infrastructure to licence such capacities. At the time of its development, there has been no appetite yet, but more recently the UK government has advanced such proposals to ensure that operators understand the theory behind flying safe, as a minimal condition for operating a drone.

The theme of unskilled piloting remains a subject of deep ambivalence in drone development, with consumer products celebrating their drone's capacity to pilot without needing technical skills, in contrast with the authority's desire to ensure that all pilots have the skills needed to control their drone in moments of failure. For example, the Fleye drone champions the autonomous capacity of its drone:

> *No piloting skills required! Fleye is really easy to use and control, using just a smartphone (iOS/ android supported). Thanks to its powerful on-board computer, Fleye is capable of executing autonomous missions for you. (Fleye Kickstarter Campaign, 2015)*

UNSIGHTED PILOTING

One of the other requirements of aviation authorities presently is that the pilot must always have *line of sight* of the drone when flying, along with the capacity for manual override of the autopilot. Yet, when the average hobbyist pilot has not undertaken a qualification to fly and, perhaps, not even established the appropriate skill set for recovery in an emergency, these rules may be quite ineffective. In part, this is why there is a wider debate about what else needs to happen in regulatory terms to ensure responsible use and minimal harms.

For all nations seeking to figure out the most appropriate level of regulation, public safety remains the key concern and there continue to be incidents, despite drone manufacturers pointing out that these are a minor proportion of the mostly successful flights that take place within the consumer sector. The problem is that any such incidents are often magnified in the press, partly due to the fact that drones represent a new, unpredictable threat to the status quo, but especially as many of the best practices of drone operations have been inadequately articulated across various sectors.

For example, in 2014, a drone was used to film a triathlon in Australia and it ended up colliding with an athlete, knocking them to the floor. The incident led to a fine of $1,700 by the Civil Aviation Safety Authority against the pilot for flying within 30 metres of people, but the entire incident raised all kinds of questions that remain unanswered about how drone usage may best be regulated. For instance, it was unclear whether the person legally responsible for the drone's operations was the same person as the pilot.

It was also unclear whether the pilot was suitably qualified to operate the drone – despite their having a licence for fixed wing aviation and having had countless hours of experience piloting. There was also ambiguity over whether the people who were close to the drone as it flew – notably, athletes and audience – could be reasonably interpreted as being under the control of the organisers, a prerequisite of flying in such circumstances. If they were, then there are greater freedoms to permit such close proximity flight. Yet, even here, there may need to be some work to explore the process by which an audience member consents to such proximity. At present – in this case and many others – this appears to be uncertain and, furthermore, difficult to establish such consent, other than indirectly asking people through some ticketed notice.

In the UK, the CAA requires that a certain level of permission is required when using a drone for any public gathering, including one that is within a gated venue, such as an open air concert or sporting event. In this case, the CAA guidelines clearly state that:

> spectators or other persons gather for sports
> or other mass public events that have not been
> specifically established for the purpose of the SUA
> operation are not regarded as being 'under the
> control of the person in charge of the aircraft'.

In such cases, additional permissions are required to undertake such aerial work. Central to these concerns is the capacity of people present to consent to being placed in a situation of risk – and this has particular impact on event organisers. For example, if an open air music festival sought to fly a drone over the concert audience, complying with the CAA (2015a) guidelines would not occur if they simply told people in attendance that there is a drone in operation around them. Rather, they state, persons at a mass public event must be able to:

> elect to participate or not to participate with the
> SUA flight operations; understand the risk posed
> to them inherent in the SUA flight operations; have
> reasonable safeguards … not have restrictions
> placed on their engagement with the purpose of
> the event or activity for which they are present if
> they do not elect to participate with the SUA flight
> operations. 3.30. (p. 40)

They go on to state more precisely that:

> it is not sufficient for persons at a public event to
> have been informed of the operations of the SUA

> *via such means as public address systems, website*
> *publishing, e-mail, test and electronic or other*
> *means of ticketing. (CAA, 2015a, p. 40)*

On occasions where such flight has occurred, it is now expected that designated take-off sites are assigned to satisfy the CAA requirements around public safety. Where no such obligations exist legally, there are good reasons for pilots to develop their own ethical flight log to ensure that a plan exists and risk assessments are undertaken, at the very least.

The Australian triathlon case also raises questions about where pilots must be located in proximity to the event, its public, and the drone itself, since the indications were that someone who tried to take the control unit undermined the pilot's control of the drone. In this case, perhaps there is a need for a pilot to be isolated from the general public or any potential threat to their being able to successful pilot the vehicle, as would be true of pilots in a cockpit. Otherwise, the present rules would prohibit any such drone flight alongside an event like a triathlon, where the general public may be close to the event space, or further measures may be required to make the drone safer or more precise. For example, the control unit could have some kind of personalised recognition system or key, which allows it to know whether the pilot has control or whether it has been taken by someone else.

Finally, the drone pilot's qualifications were in question in some of the reporting, raising questions about the circumstances that require somebody to be officially qualified to operate a drone. Indeed, in this case, there is a lack of clarity over the manner in which the drone pilot's services were employed, which has a bearing on the legality of the mission. If the drone pilot was flying commercially, then they would expect to have national qualifications, but if it were done voluntarily, as reported, then this may be governed under the rules restricting

hobbyists. In any case, the investigation into the case for pros-
ecution concluded that 'the cause of the incident was not the
actions of the operator but rather radio interference to the
UAV caused by the event's timing device' (Commonwealth
Director of Public Prosecutions, cited in Taillier, 2014).

DRONES AND PERSONAL PRIVACY

A further concern that has engaged authorities is the degree
to which camera-enabled drones have the potential to violate legal and moral expectations of personal privacy. The
UK's CAA alludes to this particularly in the context of the
privacy considerations of people who may find themselves
within the drone's camera frame. While the filming of people
in such settings with drones is subject to wider considerations
of privacy, the challenges with drones is that the practicality
of obtaining consent may be insurmountable. As such, the
CAA directs drone users to the Information Commissioner's
Office, which notes that drone films may be covered by the
Data Protection Act (2018). To this end, it encourages pilots
to consider whether drone film recordings may be capturing
moments which people would wish to be private, or avoid
sharing materials online if they may be of a sensitive nature
(Information Commissioner's Office, 2018). Yet, aside from
camera-enabled drones, it is possible that drones could be
flown and utilised to suck data from computer systems below,
hacking into networks and acquiring data without being identified and this leads to the consideration of illegal activities.

DRONES FOR DAMAGE

This section would not be complete without pointing out
the obvious way in which drones can be dangerous, which

is when they are used as weapons. Most of the examples I have mentioned in this section about the regulations governing hobby or civilian commercial use describe unintentional harms, either where harm is attributed to some kind of neglectful or irresponsible operations, or where the technology has failed to perform appropriately. However, the most obvious ways in which drones are dangerous is how they may be used intentionally to cause harm.

In Chapter 4, I consider how drones are used as weapons within military settings, but even in a civilian setting, it is a persistent concern that a drone could be flown with the expressed intent of causing harm to someone in some way. For instance, a drone could carry an explosive device, land in a crowded place and, in such a situation, it may be impossible to connect that remote flying object to a controller or operator. In this way, the prospect of drones being used for criminal activity is a tangible threat to civil order and various examples suggest a range of possibilities as to how this may transpire.

For instance, in 2015, a video appeared online originating from the USA showing a DIY drone with a handgun mounted on it. The film shows the gun discharging (although it is unclear whether a bullet or a blank is used) and this sparked a discussion about the possible misuse of drones, their vulnerability to criminal actor and the limits to which drones may be put. The video itself generated debate as to whether the creator, teenager Austin Haughwout, had broken the law simply by creating this device. Amidst widespread discussion, Haughwout subsequently released a video of a flame-throwing drone, which was shown firing a turkey to roast it. This film provoked further debate about whether the law was adequately developed to rule on such creations, to no clear conclusion (Farivar, 2016).

Beyond mechanical weapons, a drone could also be fitted with some form of biological weapon, which could be sprayed over a location as it flies, or even a projectile-based system, which could shoot towards people to cause injury. It may also be flown into people using the blades as the principal weapon, capable of all kinds of mortal injury. In this manner, the drone becomes a kind of missile, capable of completing a complex flight path and flying into something to destroy it. In each of these cases, while there may be a legal route to restriction of such applications, the challenge has been the complexity of these cases and ascertaining which is the relevant set of laws that applies. A good example of this is the ambiguity over what constitutes a commercial drone operation. In both the UK and the USA, commercial operations engage further regulations, but in the case of a video depicting drone flight, which is then subsequently posted on social media, such as YouTube, and then monetised, the content occupies a grey area in regulatory terms.

This was most widely discussed in 2015, during a US case whereby a drone operator received a letter from the FAA indicating that a complaint had been made (Koebler, 2015). The impact of this complaint relied partly on whether or not the drone film's content on YouTube could be considered a commercial product and, while the operator had not been paid to fly the drone, the monetisation of the video content on YouTube may have transformed the work into commercial activity. While even now this remains unclear, it is generally regarded that the FAA has limited interest in such matters and would only be engaged in the event of complaint. However, drone operators may leave themselves legally vulnerable, if not taking into account this potential risk.

In the UK, the CAA have made explicit references to reassure drone users that such monetised content would not typically be considered evidence of commercial activity. It states:

> *While every case should be judged on its own merits, some types of arrangements are not*

generally considered by the CAA to be commercial operations such as:

Advertising revenue received as a result of persons visiting a website or social media page where video or photographic stills shot from a UAS are displayed/posted. This is because these types of web-pages may be legitimately used to post recreational video material that was not commissioned by another party but was conceived and wholly funded by the poster. (CAA, n.d.)

THE GLOBAL PICTURE

While many nations have adopted similar principles around the regulation of drones to the USA and the UK, countries vary dramatically in their legislation and those rules also are highly dynamic, changing from one year to the next. In part, this is because there is no international standard for drone regulations, with some nations even requiring a permit for a drone to be brought into the country.

To address this variance, the United Nations (2015) established the Unmanned Aircraft Systems Advisory Group (UAS-AG), which sets out a 'Toolkit' with a number of principles for nations to consider before establishing regulatory guidelines. These consist of:

- UA may be used as toys or designed for professional users with weights ranging from the tens of grams to thousands of kilograms

- UA may carry cargo, cameras and other sensors, for example, Light Detection and Ranging (LIDAR) or infrared

- Operating modes can range from simple visual line-of-sight (VLOS) to beyond visual line-of-sight (BVLOS) operations to automatic networked swarms flying in formation. (United Nations, 2015)

It also outlines that there are some core considerations to make, which consist of remaining at a safe distance from people, buildings and airports, specifying a maximum flight height, and determining which times of day and in which weather conditions flight is permitted.

Despite these overarching principles, the rules governing drone use are still developing, with new provisions being made annually, depending on the state of the art. For instance, despite the UK's CAA championing 'line of sight' as a key operating principle for drone flights – and this being a highly regarded principle worldwide – a special exception was introduced in 2019, which allows a pilot to fly a drone while wearing FPV goggles (which prohibit visual line of sight). In doing so, the pilot is required to employ competent observers, who must be stationed across the drone's flight paths. These observers are then designated as surrogate observers, under the direction of the main pilot, who continues to assume legal responsibility. This may be the first step towards the erosion of line of sight as an operating requirement. Crucially though, this FPV provision applies only in the case of drones that do not exceed a take-off weight of 3.5 kilograms (CAA, 2019).

Additionally, as of November 2019, UK drone pilots – as for the USA's rules – are required to register their intention to fly and undertake competency tests, which will provide a legal basis for them to fly a drone. Such principles are likely to become commonplace in other countries, but there are still some tensions. For instance, the UK Government outlines a desire to avoid setting a minimum age threshold for eligibility to fly, so as not to undermine the opportunity for young people to develop STEM-related skills in their desire to fly drones. It states:

> *Age is not necessarily an indicator of competence*
> *and the Government does not want to restrict*
> *minors from piloting drones, particularly as early*
> *use of technology can build vital skills for later life,*
> *as well as introducing young people to careers in*
> *Science, Technology, Engineering and Mathematics*
> *(STEM) fields. (Department for Transport, 2019)*

As noted earlier, the problem with the present regulatory system is that the public adoption and use of drones – the ethos of drone culture – is not aligned with public expectations and a good example of this is found in the aspect to do with privacy protection. In this respect, recreational drone filmmaking is analogous to the proliferation of mobile cameras which are constantly capturing video and images of people out in the street. This is why the privacy concerns regarding drones are secondary to safety and surveillance, because of the ambiguity over what kind of personal privacy is reasonably expected in modern day living. Yet, the rules around privacy are the same for the mid-sized DJI Phantom as they are for a Hubsan nanodrone, which can fit in the palm of one's hand. These toys – some of which even come with voice control – are further examples of why the culture of drone usage is not aligned with the regulatory underpinning and this will continue to be challenging as increasingly powerful drones get increasingly smaller in size and weight.

Other key considerations have to do with a user's capacity to control their drone. Many drones today can be controlled simply via a mobile app interface on a mobile phone, cutting out many of the other technical skills associated with the traditional stick control. However, the CAA requires that pilots can demonstrate competence and that this is overseen by an independent organisation, which has the authority to confirm the pilot's ability. This means that, technically, all drone users should be trained as pilots in order to fly in a manual mode to demonstrate competence, but many people never acquire these skills, because the software makes it increasingly unnecessary.

The challenge that seems likely to emerge in future years will be over how best to apply laws in a culture where many people are ignoring them. What does a society do when it appears that the population is widely ignoring rules that are set for citizens to uphold? The first response may be to increase the policing of such infringements and set more significant penalties on infringements. A second approach is to acknowledge that the rules need to change to adjust to the emerging culture of use within society, which, in some way may reveal a change in the norms and expectations of the population around any given behaviour. Alternatively, there may be a technological solution, which would involve some kind of signal jamming technology to prevent drones from taking off in no-fly zone areas.

DESIGNING A SKYWAY

The future of airspace regulation will depend heavily on what is expected to occur around the proliferation of commercial drone services. After all, if drones are flying around our heads delivering goods or providing emergency services, then the hobbyist's capacity to fly may be further restricted to other zones. In this respect, societies must first come to terms with the changes that will occur to civilian airspace before fully understanding what may be possible for anybody else to do within densely populated zones. For some years now there have been some indications of such changes, and these may be just around the corner. In addition to Amazon's and Google's plans to operate within a drone zone, 'Airbus Skyways' is trialling 'shore to shop' drone deliveries to increase efficiencies at ports (Airbus, 2019).

While a lot remains unclear about what such a highway should look like, tests are already underway to explore the feasibility of such a system. Questions still arise as to how this network of drone flight paths would function. For example, in built up environments, it may be necessary for drones to follow similar patterns as roads to avoid the varied heights of buildings and to ensure that they are low enough to avoid other flying vehicles, and tests are underway to resolve these questions. For example, in 2017, NASA initiated a programme which explored creating a drone highway in New York, giving substance to something that previously was just an idea (Sigufsson, 2017). Furthermore, as of 2019, both Google's Wings Aviation and Amazon's Prime Air have begun deploying drone delivery systems in numerous parts of the world. Amazon's system promises a capacity to fly for up to 15 miles carrying a package of up to 5 pounds, delivering in less than 30 minutes (Rattigan, 2019). In presenting their drone to the public, Amazon describes how

> *Our newest drone design includes advances in efficiency, stability and, most importantly, in safety. It is also unique, and it advances the state of the art. How so? First, it's a hybrid design. It can do vertical takeoffs and landings – like a helicopter. And it's efficient and aerodynamic – like an airplane. It also easily transitions between these two modes – from vertical-mode to airplane mode, and back to vertical mode. It's fully shrouded for safety. The shrouds are also the wings, which makes it efficient in flight. The distinctive aircraft is controlled with six degrees*

> *of freedom, as opposed to the standard four. This*
> *makes it more stable, and capable of operating*
> *safely in more gusty wind conditions. We know*
> *customers will only feel comfortable receiving drone*
> *deliveries if they know the system is incredibly*
> *safe. So we're building a drone that isn't just safe,*
> *but independently safe, using the latest artificial*
> *intelligence (AI) technologies. (Wilke, 2019)*

Fuelling the public's imagination for future drone skyways, in 2014, Amazon also filed a patent for an 'airborne fulfilment centre', which may be broadly imagined as a flying blimp, carrying multiple UAVs, which are then deployed to locations to collect and then deliver packages. While the patent award in 2016 is real, a viral video posted in 2019 imagining the system was not, using computer-generated imagery to depict what the system might look like, once deployed. Nevertheless, the highly realistic format of the video led media outlets to describe the drone blimp as a terrifying and dystopian and treating it almost as a documentary on the future. For instance, Novak (2019) describes the discussions about the viral fake video on Twitter as 'terrifying as hell' noting how users found it to resemble some dystopian future, perhaps because it reiterates Amazon's already omnipotent status across our consumer culture. In this sense, there may yet be much to resolve about how a future drone highway operates technically and culturally, to ensure that societies are ready for them and this will have an impact on the wider utilisation of drones.

CONCLUSION: WHAT CAN WE DO WITH A DRONE?

One of the problems with resolving the regulatory issues around drone use is the clash of cultures that surrounds camera technology. The enabling impact of highly sophisticated camera technology may be completely undermined by the potential, abusive ways in which they could be used, even when the filmmaker did not intend to harm. Indeed, the same discussions about harm have taken place around the use of Google's street view cars, which are constantly mapping out our world and taking images of people within it. One of the additional challenges of this new culture of camera capture is the increasing invisibility of recording activity. Devices like Google Glass and the growing prospect of wearable technology more generally remind us how technology is getting smaller and harder to identify. When the cameras are flying above our heads, this may be even more difficult and, when one adds to this the inability to even locate the camera operator, then even the capacity to protest becomes unavailable to citizens.

This scenario is increasingly likely when factoring in the growing use of FPV goggles in drone piloting. These goggles allow the pilot to fly over greater distances with the confidence that they are able to navigate using the inbuilt camera. From the authority's perspective, this is one reason why there are calls for drones to be registered, like cars, as presently there is no way of tracing the drone to the pilot, if anything untoward were to happen. If the drone causes damage or physical harm, there may be no way of identifying who is legally responsible. Again, flying without physical line of sight is presently illegal in many countries, but the culture of such use is growing.

Nevertheless, the CAA have additional guidelines to cover the use of camera-enabled drones, which speak to people's concerns about public privacy and the ways in which cameras might be used for surveillance purposes or criminal activity. However, it is apparent that hobbyist pilots, who are part of a world where pervasive mobile device recording is the norm, are ignoring such rules. In this sense, the rules seem out of step with the cultural expectations that now describe our society. In this respect, there may be an ethical difference between the ways in which individuals take photographs and film when going about our daily lives, compared to the way in which, say, Google Street View vehicles capture content systematically around our world.

For the latter, the aggregation of data could lead to harm for citizens in terms of privacy violation, beyond simply their image captured on camera. Rather, it may be that the dataset contains meta-data, revealing such information as geographic location. Yet, large developers such as DJI are anxious to ensure that customers do not fear their data being hacked or acquired by third parties. In its website, a section titled 'Your data is none of our business', outlines a number of principles that govern its efforts to ensure robust data security within its devices, while also acknowledging its obligations to legitimate inquiries. It states:

> In the rare cases where someone is suspected of misconduct with a drone, authorities can use existing laws to investigate and prosecute wrongdoing if necessary. DJI has also deployed AeroScope, its remote identification technology, which functions as an electronic license plate for drones. Authorities can use an AeroScope receiver to obtain the serial number and pilot location of any DJI drone that raises concerns.
> (DJI Technology Inc., 2019)

Beyond potential criminal activity, the personal privacy concerns could become even more serious with the introduction of image recognition software. In April 2015, Google released details of a project that undertook image mining to produce time lapse videos of different parts of the world. Here, the system works because many thousands of people from all over the world will return to the same site at different points in time and take a photograph of the same subject. This might be a waterfall or the Grand Canyon and, by matching up images, and sequencing them over time, an animation can be created that depicts, for example, erosion or the impact of flooding, which, can tell us something about our changing world. In this case, the moral concern is less about the erosion of privacy and more about the exploitation of data, which may be utilised for commercial gain, such as more advanced marketing data. In this case, the ethical concern is not simply that recording data may violate privacy, but that sharing it within another platform will create further infringements.

Whether or not such prospects should lead us to be more cautious about the adoption of new technologies requires further interrogation, but the important point here is that the proliferation of drones foregrounds these questions. If we thought that society had problems with the saturation of mobile cameras, then the emergence of flying cameras, which are disconnected from their pilots, creates exponentially greater challenges. In this sense, drones are inextricable from the trajectory of mobile technology, intimately connected to our increasingly data-driven society and even part of the emerging discourse on wearable technologies, as might be said of the Nixie drone described earlier.

The wearable drone promises to liberate us from our geographic constraints, allowing us to document our lives as we imagine them to be, to occupy the silver screen as we intend – to be like the celebrities whose lives are constructed around elaborate productions. These devices are our gateway to a new lifestyle, where we live more adventurous, exciting lives. This is the product we are being asked to buy and the life we are being asked to celebrate. And yet, it is a life that relies on an entirely speculative proposition for many drone designs. The technology has yet to be realised, the community of customers yet to exist. Although advertising has always endeavoured to sell us a product by portraying a lifestyle the producers hope for us to find aspirational, there may be something unique about drone technology that is excessively speculative. Whereas an advert for a new car will market itself on the basis of some new, realised application the next vehicle will enjoy, drones often promise something that has yet to be fully realised technically. In this way, they are more like works of fiction than any other form of film genre.

Note

1. A full map of DJI's geographic flight restrictions, or no fly zones, is found on its website, https://www.dji.com/uk/flysafe/geo-map, providing crucial information to operators.

3

THE BRILLIANT

While the early years of the twenty-first century drone debates focussed almost exclusively on their use within military or surveillance settings, the discourse shifted considerably around 2013 towards civilian applications, which were centred on how drones were empowering citizens to occupy the sky and create films and images using their newly enabled features. The widespread excitement for drone technology since then has undoubtedly been generated by a range of the potential, humanitarian applications, which span such fields as environmental research, emergency services and healthcare provision. This chapter outlines the breadth of these uses, while also drawing attention to the many ways in which such applications are intimately connected to the drone's wider history and social value.

One of the most compelling metaphors for the humanitarian drones' movement is found within the creation of the life ring drone, a concept video for which was launched by British-based robotics company, RTS Ideas, in 2013. The film portrays a drone carrying a number of life rings out to people stranded in water, dropping them over their heads to provide critical life support. In this case, the drone is not presented as a replacement for the human lifeguard or rescuer, but is shown to be capable of attending to the emergency even more quickly, and so finds a unique place within the human/ machine configuration.

By 2015, a working prototype of a drone life ring was available, such as the *Project Ryptide* drone attachment, which raised $10,000 on Kickstarter to realise its project. By 2019, a number of drone life ring rescues have been undertaken around the world with a range of systems and yet, the drone life ring still signifies the wider aspiration among drone developers for their creations to make significant contributions to humanity's wellbeing, notably, by saving lives. Indeed, this capacity is present in many drone designs, which often seek to change the world by deploying some novel intervention to solve a problem that has no other solution.

One of the earliest examples of the burgeoning culture of enthusiasm for drone applications also has its origins in 2015, when the United Arab Emirates Prime Minister's Office launched a $1 million annual international competition for drone designers. The competition went under the title 'Drones for Good', and this motif broadly describes the aspiration of the prize to celebrate drone applications that performed a 'genuine service or present a solution to a real human need'. Among the finalists were a firefighting drone, which 'surveys the scene of a fire' to provide data that could assist decision making, a 'medical drone', which can transport medical equipment to first aid responders, and a parking attendant drone, which could monitor whether parking has been paid for or not. Others among its 800 submissions included a tree-planting drone, a window cleaning drone, a drone that can transport organs to hospitals, a waterproof drone for mapping the coral reef and coastal zones, a fog dissipation drone for driving conditions, and a drone that can identify landmines (Drones for Good, 2015).

The *national* winner of the inaugural *Drones for Good* prize was awarded to Wadi Drone, a project that 'flies over mountains and through valleys to wirelessly download photographs taken by ground-based camera traps that automatically capture images of wildlife that passes in front of the camera's motion sensor' (Wadi Drone, 2015). This application speaks to a wealth of research that is emerging around conservation drone research within the fields of environment and life sciences. For example, the *Journal of Unmanned Vehicle Systems* launched in 2013 and has since published articles that describe using aerial drones for environmental research in such areas as surveying wetlands (Chabot & Bird, 2013) using geo-referenced imagery, and deploying fixed wing vehicles to identify power line hazards for birds (Mulero-Pazmany, Negro, & Ferrer, 2013). The range of environmental drone applications is growing quickly and include such work as using drones to monitor species that are hard to locate and to track. For example, McIntosh, Holmberg, and Dann (2018) detail the process of using a drone to monitor the Australian fur seal (Arctocephalus pusillus doriferus). This paper also recognises that drones can actually disturb species too, which calls into question the legitimacy of such work. For example, they note how the drone would cause seals to look at the drone, or move towards or away from it, even attacking it at times. These considerations are crucial for researchers where there is both an ethical and scientific aspiration to ensure that the process of collecting data does not compromise the natural behaviour of the species in such a way that may distort the insights that are achieved.

Over the course of this chapter, I discuss how drones have been applied to various sectors under the banner of enriching our lives across a whole range of sectors, while also critical interrogating this narrative around contemporary drone usage. From enhancing our own personal photography or filmmaking to saving lives, drones have become imbued with the expectation to do good and, as this chapter will show, this is not coincidental. Indeed, the aspiration to re-imagine the drone is a direct response to the negative connotations that they have had and which still pervade the public's perception of how they control or destroy populations.

DRONES FOR LEISURE

As mentioned in the Introduction, in February 2015, the world's first drone film festival took place in New York, thus marking the establishment of drone cinematography as a specialist field. Historically, film festivals have always been placed where new work is presented to the public and peers, and this festival was indicative of the growing community of drone filmmakers who are steadily discovering a new kind of language through which to tell stories. The event was enabled by a crucial design feature of today's high-street drones, their on-board camera.

While, previously, aerial photography or cinematography would have been reliant on having access to a helicopter, drones democratised aerial photography, allowing many more people – with a wide range of creative ambitions – to take control of a flying camera. Indeed, where previously such activity would have been mostly a professional expertise, new drones made it possible for anybody to fly and film. Moreover, the previous years of increasing mobile technology paved the way for such desires to be nurtured. Thus, camera-enabled drones are an extension of the culture of prosumer mobile filmmaking, which has its roots in the expansion of digital cameras, camera-enabled mobile phones, and, more recently, artefacts like the selfie stick and mountable cameras made by companies like GoPro.

The public's desire to make their own films and photographs is, perhaps, the crucial way in which drones have become mass consumer devices, as is evidenced in the many promotional films made for new products. Moreover, evidence from the UK shows that 35% of recreational drone consumers purchase their drone in order to make photos and videos (CAA, 2016) and drones have been developed to specialise in such functions. Consider again the *Lily* drone, dubbed the 'selfie drone' by its developers (a tag which many subsequent drone developers have utilised).

Lily was launched in April 2015 as an investment project. Its promotional film begins with an image of a young man, high up in the mountains preparing to snowboard down the piste. The first caption reads 'Meet Lily', and immediately, the viewer is asked to think of the object not as a machine, but as an entity with a personality. The drone even has design features which resemble a face. The film then cuts to a wide shot and we are told to 'Throw and Go' Lily and, with that, the camera perspective switches to Lily's on-board camera as it follows the snowboarder down the slope. When he has finished his run, Lily automatically lands back in his hand and he is on his way. Subsequent clips include a kayaker – demonstrating Lily's waterproof functionality and its portability, and finally, we see another outdoors shot, this time showing the snowboarder's family out walking. The mother figure replicates her son's actions, throwing up Lily into the air as it flies off autonomously, filming them all enjoying a site of natural beauty. The film concludes with the family together in their living room watching back the footage captured by Lily on their TV.

Crucially, Lily does not use the word drone at all to describe itself, simply calling itself the Lily camera. This further indicates a further shift in how drones are being re-imagined through these principal, new functions. In this case, the defining feature of Lily is not that it can fly, but that it can autonomously shoot video and images from aerial perspectives, which happens to rely on its ability to fly and track a subject as it moves. It is presented as a companion to our lives, rather than an object which demands our attention or control.

The same is true of the promotional materials of many other drones, notably the 'Air Dog', also mentioned in the Introduction. Recall again how the name and promotional narrative characterises this drone as a pet dog, which will follow its master wherever they go. In this case, the promotional video shows 20–30 years old, white men, and shifts across a range of high adrenaline sports, including motor cross, surfing, wakeboarding, snowboarding, skateboarding, motorcycling and skiing.

The focus of drone promotional films on action sports may speak in part to the interests of the community of developers that surround them, rather than anything that conveys an unconscious gendered bias. Indeed, the Air Dog designers – all of whom are men – tell us that they are 'a group of innovators who are passionate about action sports' and so their promotional film endeavours to reach people like themselves: 'You don't need remote control skills. You don't need to operate the drone. You just need to concentrate on your best performance. Air Dog does the rest'. Yet, it is important to recognise that, historically, research has shown time and time again that there is an entrenched, hypermasculinity apparent in the portrayal of such activities within a range of media artefacts (Wheaton & Beal, 2003).

Unlike the development of professional drone photography and filmmaking, the uses of drones are designed to remove the need for creativity or even technical knowledge. The drone will do it all and this is expressed as a virtue of the technology, despite the fact that this also means the erosion of skilled use, which would seem to be the detriment of humanity's intelligence. Such has been the trend within amateur creative practice for some years, where mobile applications continually aspire to make the creative decisions for people in the production of media content.

Indeed, these worlds are very closely aligned. The year after the word selfie made its appearance in the Oxford Dictionary, the term 'dronie' was popularised in 2014 to describe the use of drones to create a new kind of photographic self-portrait (Jablonowski, 2014). The earliest reference to this term is found in a comment by Vimeo employee Alex Dao, in response to a Vimeo video created by Amit Gupta. The video shows Gupta filming a dronie from Bernal Hill in California (Gupta, 2014). Also in the film, standing alongside Gupta is *The New York Times* journalist Nick Bilton, who subsequently wrote about the dronie (Bilton, 2014) and Zach Klein, co-founder of Vimeo. Following the excitement generated by the video, Vimeo also created a dedicated Vimeo channel (Schroeder, 2014). If you want to establish a new meme, it helps to take along a writer from *The New York Times* and the co-founder of a major social media company!

The dronie is characterised by the act of making a self-portrait – either as a film or as a photograph – whereby the drone flies away from the subject to capture their shot. They often begin with an initial, static shot, located close to the subject, followed by a fast and lengthy zoom away, revealing a panoramic perspective of the subject's setting. Alternatively, a dronie may begin with a wide shot where the human subject is not even visible and then rapidly descend towards them – and the earth – ending with a holding shot of the person – typically the drone pilot - who is then revealed as the creator of the portrait.

While very little has been written on the dronie as a cultural or creative phenomenon, it is worth focussing on what may be going on in the establishment of this new mode of self-portraiture by scrutinising it as an artistic and cultural form. Indeed, central to this chapter's interest is the idea that drones – particularly small, multirotor drones that have become commonplace in the high street – are manifestations of humanity's desire to take back control of technology and to demonstrate control over our dominion, in a world which, increasingly, undermines human agency by ensuring any interventions within the technological system are prohibited or discouraged by the system's economic logic. The dronie is a compelling example of how people are pushing back against the closed economy of new technologies, as not only does it provide the visual evidence of the pilot exhibiting such control, it also asserts how their control is able to reveal the world to us in ways that may have not been seen before.

In this sense, there is also a desire for the dronie to evidence humanity's desire to make history through their creation of something new. To create a dronie is to undertake a radical act, not dissimilar to creative works more widely. Equally, the dronie is culturally interesting because it also undermines the focus on the self – the dronie's power is not in the eventual or initial focus on the human pilot but on the landscapes that surround them. Indeed, any landscape looks remarkable in a dronie, regardless of whether it is in a location, which might be seen as conventionally unusual or dramatic. Thus, the dronie is a decentring device, a cultural text which resists the obsession with the self that is characteristic of our contemporary, digital times. The human subject is secondary to the environment that sustains them.

The dronie creator is a skilled technologist, a creative practitioner, a socially engaged citizen, a thoughtful creator and a history maker. Some of these motifs are found within the public sharing of dronies, as is found in the Parrot #BebopYourWorld campaign from 2016. As one of the major consumer drone developers, Parrot's small quadcopters have been pioneering within this sector since its inception and have produced some of the first drones that could be found in Apple stores around the world. The core strengths of Parrot's drones consist in their ease of transportation, set up, and simple filmmaking capacities and mobility. Their Twitter campaign encouraged Bebop users to share their drone footage using such terms as #Empower-YourFreedom to characterise the expression of their work.

In this sense, the dronie is also intimately tied to the capacity to extend our lives beyond our physical limits and the drone acts as an extension of ourselves, an authentication of the value of our leisure time. It is in this sense that Jablonowski (2014) describes the power of the dronie as being a form of cultural capital:

> *The self of the selfie is the self that is trying to sovereignly manage the authenticating view of itself. The self of the dronie, in turn, is the self that is trying to sovereignly manage the aerial view. Air power could therefore also perhaps be understood as a form of cultural capital.*

DRONE RACING

Another exciting arena to have developed in the era of the modern multirotor drone is drone racing. While the practice has quite humble roots dating back to around the same time quadcopters became widely available, with amateur drone enthusiasts experimenting with DIY platforms, there has been a surge of large-scale competitive events since then. Today, drone races are staged in huge arenas around the world and, in a remarkably short space of time, the sport has gone through a process of codification, which has standardised rules for competition and generated big prize money events.

Central to the practice of drone racing is the first person view (FPV) format, which involves the pilot using goggles that relay a video feed from their drone's on-board camera, creating the sense of being seated inside the cockpit of their drone. This also means that the pilot can only see what the drone's camera reveals, rather than its broader location in space. As the drone's camera feed uses radio signals to send content into the goggles, this means that spectators can also use their own goggles and tune into the same frequency to experience the feeling of being on the drone too. It also allows them to switch from one drone perspective to another by changing their radio frequency, to follow their favourite racer. Consequently, drone racing also provides an insight into the transformation of sports spectatorship that is occurring as a result of new technologies. Increasingly, sports fans expect to be part of the field of play, rather than just be onlookers into its activity. Drone racing exemplifies this principle most effectively, providing personalised spectator experiences.

Closely related to this is one of the most exciting aspects of drone racing, which is the staging of the events. Drone racing has become an entirely new theatre of sporting spectacle, re-imagining the conventional arena through the drone's occupation of varying altitudes within the physical space. One of the fascinating discussions facing the future of drone racing has to do with the way in which it marries together the kinds of innovations that one would expect to see alongside Formula 1 racing with the integration of artificially intelligent machines capable of self-direction, but where the control interface is similar to the latest computer games consoles. In fact, in 2019, the Drone Champions League released a drone racing computer game, which allows players to control a drone in graphical versions of real-world track, even using their drone controller within the game.

What will be especially interesting to investigate in the future is the degree to which this simulated experience mirrors the physical world drone piloting skills. Potentially, gaming drone experiences will be ideal training grounds for real-world drone racing, liberating people from their geographical limitations, but also creating opportunities to compete in ever more fantastical virtual arenas. In this respect, drone racing is pioneering the convergence of various industries and interfaces that reveal new directions in human endeavour.

CONSERVATION DRONES

Moving away from the use of drones for sport and leisure, the wider utility of drones for scientific research has become a key dimension of their wider social value. In fact, innovation research is at the heart of many drone achievements, whether or not their public appreciation is found within a scholarly context. A good example is the work at ETH Zurich, which has involved collaboration with artists, drone racing, and a range of other cultural activities. Scientific research projects have become a key feature of the drones for good narrative, not least because they are often intimately connected to developing remarkable artefacts of public consumption, notably extraordinary films which portray the natural world in ways that have never been seen before.

For instance, in 2015, National Geographic produced a film outlining a project that utilised drones to further our understanding of what happens within an active volcano (National Geographic, 2015). In this case, set on the island of Vanuatu, the artefacts created through such work are the film, but also the data captured, which researchers explain as providing ground-breaking insights into what happens inside an active volcano. The extraordinary footage captured by the drone's on-board camera, also occupies the space of cinematographic achievements. Indeed, the lead creator in the film, Sam Crossman, is introduced as an 'Explorer and Filmmaker'.

While Crossman's credentials as a scientist are not well articulated within the public materials for the National Geographic project, the team that accompanied him included geobiologist Jeffrey Marlow, who explains the project team's scientific expertise. He describes how the drone's value as a research tool is found in its being able to capture data that can later be used to analyse what is happening within the volcano. He further explains how the drone footage reveals crucial insights into the emergence of microbial colonies on the newly cooled rock, enriching our understanding of how life emerges more widely on planet Earth.

The example is a helpful insight into the range of skills needed to undertake drone research, a key component of which is having great, creative filmmaking skills to ensure impact and appreciation in society more widely. One of the great appeals of drones for research is found in their capacity to host a whole range of sensors and devices – such as cameras or thermal imaging devices – which permit the capture of data that can then be used to better understand the natural world.

Drones also offer an affordable and efficient way for scientists to survey areas for evidence of environmental change or wildlife behaviour (Colomina & Molina, 2014). From using drones to fly over treetops in the Brazilian rainforest to monitor the behaviour of primates (Wich & Koh, 2018), to flying over estuaries to identify areas of erosion or river flow (Entwistle, Heritage, & Milan, 2019), the rise of conservation drones has become a transformative practice in environmental research, helping to reveal insights into the natural world that have previously been unattainable without significant financial investment. Before UAVs, only helicopters could be used and these would not be helpful in situations where a smaller vehicle is required. Thus, the rise of micro-drones is enabling a new research community to emerge, much of which is focussed on improving our understanding of the natural world.

The main values of such drone-enabled research fall into four categories. First, they can improve the efficiency of research insights, either in terms of the economic cost of undertaking such work or the amount of time required to do it and, of course, these two are closely related. For example, drones can often map a terrain at a speed that exceeds any other existing means. In turn, this can decrease the time a researcher needs to make an assessment of a geographic location. Second, drones for research can increase the accuracy of research findings, either because they allow researchers to access data that is otherwise impossible to reach or by providing an affordable means by which researchers can undertake multiple data capture intervals. Third, data gathering drones can generate additional insights that derive from the aggregation of that data. This is not unique to a drone's capacity, but drones lead the way in the potential to use such methods as photogrammetry to make more sense of our world, as was used in the research from Vanuatu.

Finally, drones are capable of deploying novel data acquisition devices to acquire data where there are no alternatives available. A great example here is the project that collects 'whale snot' by flying the 'Snotbot' drone over a whale as it exhales through its blowhole. A petri dish located on the drone is moved into position, collecting a sample as the spray of water and snot flies into the sky. One of the crucial values of this work – which launched a Kickstarter campaign 2015 – is that it obtains samples from healthy subjects, whereas previous findings have relied mostly on collecting data from already unhealthy individuals, such as stranded animals. In this sense, the UAV solution can provide a clearer understanding of the state of the health of animal populations (Geoghegan et al., 2018).

Undoubtedly then, the most exciting area of scientific research that are enabled through drone technology are found within the environmental and life sciences – research that takes place in the natural world, where drones can roam freely and explore areas that otherwise would be impossible to reach. However, outside of the environmental sciences, drones have also found applications in a range of other settings, which are instrumental to sustainability goals. For instance, agricultural drones are used by farmers to count livestock, monitor crops and undertake aerial seeding. This is helpful especially in places of high vulnerability, where identifying the optimal places for planting is crucial. For example, in 2018, as part of the USA's 'Feed the Future' programme, researcher Jon Carroll led a team experimenting with drones to monitor crop vitality (AUVSI, 2018). The project team explains how:

> The drone captures images with special cameras
> that allow researchers to quantify how much water
> and chlorophyll is in the plants. It also allows for
> 3-D measurements of plants in different parts
> of the field. Based on this data, researchers can
> recommend potential solutions to low crop yields.
> (Oakland University, 2018)

One of the big challenges in conducting such work is establishing principles of best practice. Drones continue to be quite noisy and likely to disturb wildlife. Thus, in the absence of clear, species specific guidelines, it is possible that research could be damaging or deterimentally affecting the behaviour of animal life. In this sense, it is crucial that environmental researchers plan out projects with these kinds of risks in mind, with a view to establishing optimal operating principles for missions. For example, Callaghan, Brandis, Lyons, Ryall, and Kingsford (2018) outline various risks associated with monitoring nesting waterbirds, setting out principles for the least intrusive investigations.

More widely, Hodgson and Koh (2016) outline a number of principles to maximise the ethical conduct of research. Their guidelines span adherence to wider conventions in ethical drone practice – such as domestic aviation rules. This is important especially as beliefs vary on the freedom of academic researchers to undertake their work. While it may be presumed that academic research is not subject to the same restrictions that may govern commercial drone use, in many countries this has no legal basis and researchers may find themselves in difficulty, if they are not aware of their legal obligations before taking flight. The guidelines offered by Hodgson and Koh (2016) also specify the need to select appropriate equipment (e.g. fixed wing vs. multirotor), minimising wildlife disturbance, ceasing operations if disturbance occurs and detailed methodological reports on the protocols used in the flight.

Overall, whether it is through the use of photogrammetry or remote sensing, environmental drones are making a big impact on the conduct of research, but there is a lot more work needed to ensure these applications are effective, ethical and reliable.

DRONES FOR HEALTH

While the health of the natural world is becoming better understood through the use of drones for research, the same is true also of human health. Since the early designs of twenty-first century micro-drone uses, health applications have been imagined, with one of the most well-discussed being the 'drone ambulance', a flying defibrillator, designed to attend to an emergency situation, as quickly as possible. In a concept video from 2014, designer and master's student at the

University of Delft (2014), Alec Moment, revealed how his drone ambulance could be equipped with a direct audio feed so that the healthcare professional could speak to a person on site and guide them to use the defibrillator and provide a time critical service, where there may be no other solution.

Since then, the drone ambulance has found many alternative applications, such as the delivery of human biological products. For example, since 2016, USA start-up *Zipline* has developed a delivery system that is servicing Rwanda and Ghana and, in 2017, conducted its first life-saving delivery mission. In 2016, the Rwandan Ministry of Health (2018) reported how its drone delivery system had resulted in 3,246 deliveries with 929 emergency deliveries taking place. Baker (2017) describes how Zipline has reduced blood delivery times from 3 hours to 15 minutes and that the Rwandan approach to regulating air space is now informing the USA's approach to bring similar services into the country. Among the considerations in deploying such a system are matters of liability, hacking and the potential patient education transfer which may not occur without a face-to-face consultation (Lin, Shah, Mauntel, & Shah, 2018).

At the University of Central Lancashire in the UK, researchers have explored the potential of using a gesture control interface that would allow patients to undertake a range of movements that can assist with their muscular rehabilitation after injury. Moving around one's arms to control the movement of a drone extends this capacity. Early development around such use took place also in 2013 when Marin Fortsch and Thomas Endres developed an application for a Parrot AR.Drone that used a 3-D camera and wifi to control a drone with just arm movements (Fortsch, 2014). This application extends the recent trend towards the integration of gaming tasks within rehabilitative healthcare, which is predicated on the recognition that such behaviours incentivise patients to exercise more and, thus, significantly improve the rate at which improvements occur. Indeed, crossing these two worlds, Samsung Electronics recently was awarded a patent for a gesture-based interface for a drone design (Beomshik Kim, 2018) and, in 2017, the DJI Spark came packaged with gesture control for photography.

DRONE JOURNALISM

As platforms of investigation, drones have also become popular tools for journalists. Indeed, Strong and Zafra (2016) describe drones as critical components of an emerging era of 'backpack journalism', which encompasses other technological systems, such as mobile recording and data-driven journalism. Some of the most remarkable examples of drone journalism are found within circumstances of extreme difficulty, such as natural disasters or other emergency situations. There is now nearly no catastrophic event around the world which is not covered by a drone journalist in some way.

The appeal of drones within journalism is unambiguous in such circumstances. Drones can be deployed rapidly, they are cost-effective, safer than being physically present, but also provide extraordinary visual materials which make for compelling content through which to engage audiences. Yet, drones also function as ideological tools, making manifest the journalist's aspiration to report on events that, otherwise, might be hidden or restricted from public view, in service of governmental control. Indeed, in many circumstances, using a drone is not a simple exercise, as there are restrictions on their use by aviation authorities. In this respect, a journalist may be acting unlawfully in their news coverage without having first obtained the appropriate permissions and, yet, the drone can be a critical tool especially in countries where there are numerous restrictions on media freedom. A good example of this is found in the journalist practice and community work of AfricanDRONE.

Set up as a grassroots organisation, AfricanDRONE 'seeks to empower the drone pioneers already living on the continent, by networking them together into a self-help association that can share resources and knowledge' Africa Drone (no date). In doing so, it pursues 'stories that tackle social justice or development issues – urbanisation, civic organisation, climate change and global migration' and asks its reporters to champion principles of 'open data', mentoring and becoming a member of its community.

In Nairobi, Hammertsin and Niranjan (2018) report how journalists have used drones to call government reporting into question and to verify what is going on in countries where media freedom does not exist.

> *For Nairobi-based journalist Soila Kenya, technology is a tool to unearth the truth. She recounts an attack by terrorist group al-Shabab in 2018, when militants struck an army base in Kulbiyow, Somalia. Kenya's defense forces downplayed the damage and claimed they had repelled the attackers. But satellite stills and drone footage told a different tale. Analysts from African Defense Review and research group Bellingcat found militants had in fact overrun the base – and inflicted heavy casualties in the process. Satellite technology unearthed something that 'really would not have been possible otherwise', said Kenya.*

The continued use of drones within journalism cannot be taken for granted, as the ambiguity of legal restrictions are open to exploitation and are becoming more rigorously enforced around the world. For example, in 2015, the Kenyan

Government effectively grounded the journalist community African SkyCam (Professional Society for Drone Journalists, 2015).

Increasingly, when using a drone for any purpose within civilian airspace, the drone pilot may be subject to certain restrictions, such as needing to obtain permission to fly or having a legally recognised national qualification. Here, one can see how legislation around drone use may be incompatible with other social priorities, such as certain principles that we would seek to be free from any kind of governmental restriction. A journalist enjoys a certain kind of freedom because their work produces information that is in the public interest; drones, because their use is more restricted compared to other journalist's tools, may limit the capacity to undertake journalism that is free from unreasonable restrictions from offices of power. Such restrictions may be interpreted as an assault on free speech as Holton, Lawson, and Love (2015) describes in the context of FAA restrictions:

> *The FFA's [sic.] commercial ban acts to single out journalists, effectively barring them from sources of information available to the general public. For example, if a hobbyist and a journalist both flew the same flight pattern and recorded the same images, the FAA would find that the journalist's flight was illegal but the hobbyist's was not. The sole distinction between the two is that the journalist, by accepting compensation, somehow receives lesser protection under the First Amendment. Such a result is clearly counter to constitutional norms.*

Here, again, there are points in common between the drone and other forms of communication technology. The printing press was similarly radical in its capacity to allow anybody to publish material on a large scale, whether or not it was approved by the state. The same may be true of the internet, where discussions continue to take place about the extent to which it should be regulated by some kind of governmental agency. Indeed, such discussions have been heightened in the context of debates about fake news debates and the proliferation of offensive material online.

In some sense, as a manifestation of creative innovation within the practice of journalism, the drone speaks to the fact that there is no technology out there that is value free at the point of application. Technology always engages a range of values, many of which may be in tension with each other. In this case, the drone provides the capacity to traverse the restricted, contested views of the people on the streets whose ground-level perspectives make it impossible to verify the truth. By flying above everyone, the drone assumes the authoritative, objective position.

Among the many questions that follow on from the emergence of a new cultural and professional practice is whether it constitutes a change in degree or a change in kind. In the case of drones, as for all other formats of media innovation within journalism, the question is whether the drone journalist is a new kind of journalist, represents a new kind of journalism, or whether the drone is simply another component in a journalist's toolkit. Resolving such matters requires careful understanding of what it is to undertake drone journalism, but so too does it require understanding how such work exists within the broader practices and processes that govern journalism as an industry. It is tempting to claim that drones are just another means through which to undertake journalism, but it is clear that the possibility of documenting the world from above brings an entirely new perspective on the act of journalism. At the very least, drones give rise to the emergence of new communities of journalists who focus their time and energy on stories that are made possible only by and through the creation of drones.

While drones have created a new branch within the journalist community, drone journalism does not negate the need for other forms of journalism or diminish the importance of other methodologies for documenting the world. One could quite reasonably pursue a career as a drone journalist in the same way that one could become an online journalist, or an Instagram journalist or a Facebook journalist, or a printed newspaper journalist. Also while we often think about a journalist's obligation as needing to occupy all platforms at all times, it is clear that the practice of drone journalism requires deep investment. Learning to fly a drone is a very different kind of commitment to learning to use Twitter.

To outline these challenges more fully, the Professional Society of Drone Journalists provides extensive guidance on the issues confronting journalist drone pilots. Notably, its Code of Ethics for Drone Journalism sets out a hierarchy of considerations which may govern decisions about when and how to use a drone in the name of journalism:

1. Newsworthiness. *The investigation must be of sufficient journalistic importance to risk using a potentially harmful aerial vehicle. Do not use a drone if the information can be gathered by other safer means.*

2. Safety. *A drone operator must first be adequately trained in the operation of his or her equipment. The equipment itself must be in a condition suitable for safe and controlled flight. Additionally, the drone must not be flown in weather conditions that exceed the limits of the drone's ability to operate safely, and it must be flown in a manner that ensures the safety of the public.*

3. Sanctity of law and public spaces. *A drone operator must abide by the regulations that apply to the airspace where the drone is operated whenever possible. An exception to this is provided in instances where journalists are unfairly blocked from using drones to provide critical information in accordance with their duties as members of the fourth estate. The drone must be operated in a manner which is least disruptive to the general population in a public setting.*

4. Privacy. *The drone must be operated in a fashion that does not needlessly compromise the privacy of non-public figures. If at all possible, record only images of activities in public spaces, and censor or redact images of private individuals in private spaces that occur beyond the scope of the investigation.*

5. Traditional ethics. *As outlined by professional codes of conduct for journalists. (PSDJ, 2015)*

While the Society website is less active than it once was, its documents reveal the origin story of the professional drone journalism community. Indeed, since then one can find drone journalism codes for journalists at national levels, which outline key principles in best practice for drone journalists to follow. For example, in 2017, a collaboration between a number of organisations in the USA, including the National Press Photographers Association, developed best practice guidelines that it considers need to be 'even more stringent than other journalism ethics'. While there is no official mandating of these guidelines, the contributing partners advance them as a guide to operating ethically as drone journalists and the principles encompass the following areas: flying safely, respecting the law, respecting privacy, being cautious to not disrupt events, not overly editorialising content through special effects, ensuring pilot autonomy in decision making, rigorous and regular training of piloting skills and sharing among peers to grow an ethically aware drone journalism community (Drone Journalism Code of Ethics, 2017).

The drone journalist is still someone who operates at the margins of professional journalism. Within a series of interviews with drone journalists, Belair-Gagnon, Owen, and Holton (2017) describe how 'individuals inside newsrooms who did not necessarily identify as journalists were given the freedom to experiment with an emerging technology on the bounds of acceptable practice' (p. 1367). In turn, their interventions are disrupting established forms of journalism (Gynnild, 2014). Moreover, through their practice, drone journalists are establishing new norms among journalist practice, along with changing expectations from audiences who now anticipate the drone's eye view in coverage of world events.

CONCLUSION

In sum, these 'brilliant' applications of drones serve a range of purposes for societies, from fulfilling complex ideological aspirations, to providing sources of entertainment. Yet, it is important to be vigilant about why the public discourse on drones has shifted from anxiety to aspiration. Furthermore, it is crucial that one debates the overall merit of such a transformation. This is because the 'Drones for Good' narrative may obscure a number of atrocities undertaken by drone and the intimate relationship between such innovations and the consumer technologies that may derive from such achievements. In this sense, one may argue that the introduction of autonomous drones into civilian contexts could lead to a more permissive culture of use in more politically contentious contexts, such as conflict environments.

One of the biggest challenges with autonomous machines is understanding where one can locate human agency – if at all. It is possible to identify such agency in semi-autonomous machines, where the human programmer's intentions are evidenced. However, it is much harder to do so where the programmer is not required, or where an initial algorithm or set of learned principles leads to additional discovery and new learning, which was not previously imagined by the programmer. In this sense, introducing autonomous machines into society may provide something of a litmus test for public opinion and some indication as to how complex societies can cope with such devices.

The more contested consequence of the 'Drones for Good' programme is that it may also be a context that provides additional opportunities for military-based companies to extend their revenue by reaching a civil population. This is alarming since, as the technology develops, it becomes increasingly reliant on the innovative leaps made within the military context. In this sense, the commercial, civil revenue can be a catalyst for innovation that feeds military applications, either in terms of technology or simply economic investment. The desirability of such circumstances will feature in the next chapter, which examines the 'bad' applications of drone technology.

4

THE BAD

Despite applications of drone technology for humanitarian or social good, the longer history of drones is awash with applications, the purpose of which is to defend, destroy or control people and civilisations. Among the earliest examples in modern times is the US Predator drone (which developed into the Atomics MQ-9 Reaper), the arrival of which signalled the moment when drones became part of the public consciousness. While initially used for surveillance, the Predator rose to prominence after 9/11 when its operations were given approval for destructive missions, justified by political leaders within the context of the new war on terror (Mayer, 2009).

This chapter addresses what has happened since the emergence of such applications, where drones have been used to bring about harm, exploring the overlap between civilian, military and policing applications. It focusses especially on the military context to examine what it means for humanity to seek further absence from the field of combat. Moreover, it investigates the societal implications of undertaking devastating acts of violence from remote locations, while also addressing broader questions of human relationships that are at stake in such an era.

It is first crucial to understand that, since the Predator, the recent history of drone advocacy has seen a distancing from these applications. Indeed, Chapman's comment cited earlier about how the older generation of drone developers are shying away from their use of the word 'drone', favouring instead the acronym UAV, reflects an attempt from within the drone industry to distance itself from these controversial historical origins. This manoeuvre speaks to the wider, intimate relationship between military aspirations and technological innovation. In many instances, there may not have been a scientific or technological breakthrough that has changed the world for the better without there first having been some form of investment that was designed to support national, military interests. Whether this trade-off can be morally justified depends partly on how such military interests are characterised – to strengthen defence, or to achieve more effective means of attack.

In any case, it is useful to inquire into the consequences of this gambit, whereby civilian innovation is enabled by military research, which raises a number of crucial questions. For instance, what are the compromises we make morally by accepting the trade-off between military and civilian innovation? Alternatively, how else might societies stimulate technological innovation, without the need to become entangled with the large financial investments made in the name of defence? Are there limits to such an innovation chain, or might we also need to bring certain kinds of militaristic innovation to an end, despite it leaving us vulnerable to other nations, which may not undertake such limitations?

This is precisely the discourse that operates around nuclear weapons and this chapter examines the complexity of these arguments in the context of drones. It considers whether humanity is better with drones or without them, when we know that their development - and the many humanitarian applications that exist now - are enabled by humanity's more nefarious aspirations. These are not simple questions to answer, but it is crucial to understand the relationship between technological innovation and societal structures to answer them adequately. To do so, we will first examine how drones provide insight into these relationships.

DRONE WARFARE

The relationship between military technology and wider societal technological change is complex and multifaceted. At times, military research gives society amazing technologies, such as the internet, which has its roots partially in the USA's Department of Defense and its Advanced Research Projects Agency Network programme. In other situations, the military may utilise scientific and technological discoveries to create weapons that appear to make life on Earth more precarious, as might be said of atomic weapons or nuclear missile technology.

One of the challenges with finding moral resolution to the trajectory of technology is that the principal ambition of such research pivots on a dubious interpretation of the military's social role. In one interpretation, the military's function is to provide the means of defending a nation, while on another it serves to subject other nations to its will. A further, morally dubious dimension to military intervention is their fundamentally unpredictable impact. Even when the intentions of military interventions have somewhat justifiable underpinnings, there may be unintended consequences to such actions that frustrate the realisation of such goals. We see this time and again when nations endeavour to rid another nation of violent dictators through deploying military personnel, only to create situations of considerable disruption and other forms of harm.

Regardless of one's position on the merits of military inter-ventions in an absolute sense, it is unequivocal that military aspirations are intimately tied to technological advances. After all, ownership of technological innovation in weaponry leads to military advantage. In this respect, drones are consist-ent with the historical interpretation of technological change, which indicates that major international competitive advan-tage economically is intimately connected to military innova-tions. Indeed, such rhetoric about this close relationship is a persistent feature of government investment into technologi-cal culture. Consider how the British Government's Secretary of State for Defence articulates its orientation towards nur-turing an innovation culture:

> *This battle-winning technology supplies better intelligence, delivers greater precision and ensures better situational awareness, all things that are vital to mission success in Afghanistan and essential to our efforts to safeguard the local population. (Hammond, 2013)*

This perspective on the importance of technological inno-vation is reiterated time after time with the subsequent British Government Secretary of State for Defence stating that:

> *Our adversaries, whether state or non-state, are increasingly harnessing new technologies and unconventional methods against us .... Advantage through Innovation aims to maintain the military edge of the UK's Armed Forces into the decade ahead and beyond. (Fallon, in Ministry of Defence, 2016)*

In this analysis, the government paper uses the Skeeter Dragonfly UAV as a case study to exemplify how innovation drives advantage. The dragonfly's objectives are to increase capacity around 'intelligence, surveillance, and reconnaissance' (Ministry of Defence, 2016, p. 12), and to function in urban spaces.

In this application, one can also observe the intimate connection between scientific research and the eventual, technological applications to military projects. Underpinning the Skeeter Dragonfly UAV is the scientific research of Thomas, Taylor, Srygley, Nudds, and Bomphrey (2004), which examines the remarkable evolutionary achievements of the dragonfly's airframe. The research seeks to explain, biomechanically, how such flight is achieved, but not necessarily for any human application:

> *One major implication of this result is that the root-flapping motion characteristic of all flying animals may be a constraint, imposed by the pre-existing musculo-skeletal structure, rather than an adaptation.*

In this simple statement, it is apparent how the research seeks to design technology which takes the best principles from nature and then endeavours to improve upon them by removing evolutionary constraints. Yet, insights from such work have found eventual application in the design of the Skeeter, which has sought to optimise flight time for surveillance missions. The Skeeter drone is cited in Fallon's (2016) military report on drones, but, for the scientists behind the work, their aspirations extend beyond such applications:

> *Skeeter also has uses in search and rescue, surveying, and agriculture; and in particular where small-scale hovering UAS with high gust tolerance, high speed and greater endurance are required (Animal Dynamics, 2019).*

If one is at all anxious about the work of scientists whose work finds application within military contexts, then it may be some consolation to imagine that there is an eventual trickle down of innovation from the military to societal goods. However, one reason to be cautious about this way of rationalising the morality of technological innovation is the potential for the civilian market to become integral to the further advances of military interests. For example, the Russian tank, named the Kurganets-25, uses a control system that resembles a PlayStation control pad. The Vice President of the vehicle's manufacturer, Albert Bakov, explains in the Russian government owned media platform (Sputnik International, 2015) that:

> *I spent two years on convincing the designers to make the console similar to a Sony PlayStation gamepad, to make it easier for a young soldier to familiarize himself with it.*

This example reveals what is especially controversial about the rise of drones and why discussions about drones attract such public debate. The explanation for this is located in the principles of design and may, in fact, mean that civilian innovation also works towards the achievement of military ambitions. This is especially true as the practice of designing simulations becomes intimately connected to how people learn within simulators in such a way as to transfer into a range of contexts. To elaborate on this, it is useful to examine in more detail the trajectory of simulation design.

DESIGNING OUT REALITY

As simulation technology develops, it gravitates towards a seamless mirroring of the physical world, leading to a point where they become indistinguishable. We have seen it many times in the movies, where a virtual reality is imperceptibly different from an actual physical reality. In circumstances, where designers have perfected the art of simulation, the virtual world ceases to be a training ground for some other reality. Instead, the two worlds become indistinguishable. The consequence of this may be a limitation of our capacity to make moral distinctions between acts that occur within the simulation and acts that occur outside of it. The simulation becomes the principal reality in which we live out our lives.

The growing alignment of simulation and game playing creates further moral discomfort, especially when actions within the simulation resemble acts that would, otherwise, be deemed deeply immoral, such as the act of killing within a computer game. Indeed, the moral panic surrounding violent computer games is a consequence of such anxieties – of not knowing whether the increasingly realistic game, in some ways, has implications for how people make sense of the world beyond the game. In the main part, the public discourse on such subjects takes place outside of the realm of contested evidence and much more at the level of intuition.

Leaving this aside for a moment, the key point for our discussion is that humanity is approaching, what Baudrillard describes as the point at which the simulation becomes the reality. The act of game playing, enabled by the design interface being modelled on a PlayStation control system, is a further step towards gamifying war, but, most nefariously, involving civilians in the process towards such work. The Kurganets-25 brings into an uncomfortable juxtaposition the most serious of human behaviours (acts within war) with a pursuit that is culturally located in the sphere of playful behaviour (gaming activities).

The even more troubling dimension of this alignment is the idea that young people, or even children, might be

acquiring skills through their leisure, which have direct trans-
ferability into a military context. Their interrelations hints at
a future where the most qualified military weapons operators
could be children, since they may also be the best computer
games players. Indeed, Bakov's (cited in Sputnik International, 2015) reference to how the design interface will be more
intuitive for younger soldiers, who have grown up as gamers,
establishes this association. In doing so, it institutes a way of
thinking about gaming that, subsequently, becomes inextrica-
bly linked to the potential transfer to military interventions
and the implications of this are deeply profound. This may be
especially true in an era of drone warfare.

For instance, let us suppose that being a good gamer means
also having developed the technical skills that are optimal for
drone operations. One dilemma arising from such circumstances concerns the matter of deciding when it is appropriate
to assist a child in coming to terms with this association. This
is especially important if the design of gaming experiences
becomes aligned with the wider aspiration to optimise the
skill set of future military personnel. What troubles us morally about this relationship is the prospect that game design
may become aligned with military interests generally and skill
development specifically, or that there may even be a synergy
between the two. In such circumstances, one might imagine a
situation whereby some military regime seeks to exploit the
talent of young gamers by putting them into a context where
their gaming activity feeds into servicing military objectives,
perhaps even without their realising this.

Such ideas are played out in Card's (1985) science fiction
novel *Ender's Game*, along with its 2013 film adaptation
(Brandt, 2013), which

> *tells the story of a young boy at an elite military*
> *academy. Set several decades after a terrible*

war between humans and an alien race called
the buggers, the novel follows the life of a boy
named Ender. At age 6, recruiters take Andrew
'Ender' Wiggin from his family to begin military
training. He excels in all areas and eventually
enters officer training. There he encounters a new
video game-like simulator in which he commands
spaceship battalions against increasingly complex
configurations of bugger ships.

Ender describes his journey in the following terms:

The International Fleet decided that the world's
smartest children are the planet's best hope. Raised
on war games, their decisions are intuitive, decisive,
fearless. I am one of those recruits. (Script from
film)

This story gets to the root of what often creates alarm about drones, which have become synonymous with the dehumanising effects of technological adoption and wider anxieties about the power of machines to bring humanity into their service. *Ender's Game* imagines a future which has gone wrong in terrible ways, particularly with regards to its exploitation of the most vulnerable civilians in the service of some supposedly just cause, which amounts, essentially, to a pursuit of self-preservation.

When Ender questions the justification of his training in the pursuit of war, his commander indicates that 'The purpose of this war is to prevent all future wars' (Hood, 2013) and we see a similar rhetoric around the development of nuclear weapons. Those nations who have nuclear weapons justify their creation as a deterrent to others who may seek to invoke their use as part of military interventions. In this regard, these ultimate weapons of mass destruction are justified on the basis that we seek never to use them. However, one of the weaknesses of such reasoning in the context of *Ender's Game* is that the solution enters the world of children. In this way, the story takes us even further down a road that is ridden with morally dubious decision making. The protected realm of childhood is destroyed by the application of the desire to seek power, control and dominance.

Even worse than this is the fact that the exploitation involves misleading children into believing that their military training is all mere simulation. As the story unfolds, it is subsequently revealed that the game is the actual conflict, where actual lives were lost. As Brandt (2013) describes, Ender is devastated by this news, but the case proves that situating soldiers in a context that they believe to be a simulation may be the most effective means of engaging them productively in the battle field. By implication, the drone pilot who is able to distance him/herself from the real lives that are lost or destruction that is bought by their actions may be the most effective soldier.

While it is tempting to dismiss fiction as just a story, Harmon (2003) reports that these ideas correspond with military strategies and that the wider employment of electronic games is already critical to simulation training for soldiers. Moreover, Guedim (2017) reports that gaming is already used by the US Army as a recruitment and grooming device and, in 2002, launched its own official computer game available on gaming platform, Steam. In this respect, drones represent a significant step in a direction that we, subsequently, may wish had never been taken. One might even imagine that young gamers looking for a way to transfer their skills into some kind of career path will, in fact, gravitate towards the military where they may believe that such gaming skills are valued. In this sense, Sputnik International's (2015) Russian tank story may, in fact, be interpreted as a form of recruitment propaganda for a youth that is intimately involved with gaming culture.

The story tells the reader that gamers have a role to play in Russian military operations.

Drones take such dystopian principles to a new level and are associated with a new kind of warfare, the impact of which has its roots in the 1990s, when Jean Baudrillard wrote about the first Iraq war not having happened. In making this controversial assertion, Baudrillard was alluding to the idea that the war was fought through a series of simulation interfaces and through media spectacle, which made it more like a computer game than warfare. He considered that, due to it being fought at a distance, with remote missiles being targeted from well outside of the field of conflict, war had become something very different from what it had been over humanity's entire history before that point. While Gregory (2011) rejects the comparison of gaming to drone warfare, the dismissal is based on the contextualisation of these different acts and we must be mindful of the long-term shift that seems to be an inevitable consequence of designing increasingly realistic simulators.

While I have no doubt that the vast majority of playstation gamers engaged in war games understand that their acts do not bring about physical harm to real people, the drone pilot appreciates that their own acts do have significant consequences. Yet, in neither case can one reject the proposition that the skill requirements of each task have common ground. Imagine if, as is true of football computer games, the millions of war-based computer games could be utilised as forms of modelling different military situations, where the data generated by players provide some insight into how to act tactically within a military setting. In this case, it is not simply the skill acquisition and its translation from leisure to defence that may trouble us. Rather, it is the less apparent exploitation of data from gaming experiences and its use by the military that may be the more alarming, immediate implication.

THE ABSENCE OF HUMANITY

One of the most symbolically troubling aspects of drone technology is the way in which it represents the gradual erosion of
the human within social endeavours. In this respect, the consideration of drone warfare has great value, because it places
the weight of such removal into the most grave of contexts,
namely the destruction of human life. The drone, in its singular act of complete annihilation within warfare, is a warning
to society of a wider cultural phenomenon, which involves
the eradication of human existence through the increased
remoteness of our interactions. The drone pilot is alone in
their pursuit of destruction. Yet, they are also part of a col-
lection of other actors who are undertaking similar acts. In
this sense, the drone is emblematic of a society which, despite
becoming more global, or more digitally connected, is also
becoming constituted by individuals who are more isolated
from each other physically, emotionally and morally. Alone,
together, as Turkle (2017) describes.

As with any new technological development, it can be very
difficult to ascertain the long-term impacts of the changes it
generates and, often, once such change has occurred, it is then
too late to do very much about it. Consider the environmental
damage caused by the automobile, itself now in the midst of
a technological revolution set to create sustainable transportation. At the beginning of this vehicular revolution, it was
not just that foresight was not available, but that matters of
environmental concern were not in circulation. This is why
it is essential that one looks to stories to give us insights into
where technology may take humanity, as it is there where
one may locate ideas that are not yet found within the socio-
political sphere. Some of our most compelling insights into
the impact of such circumstances are found – sometimes, only
found – within fiction.

For drones, the impacts of a world of drone warfare are told especially well in the arthouse film, '5000 Feet is the Best' (Fast, 2011), which is structured around two, interwoven stories. One of the stories is a fictionalised conversation between a journalist and a drone pilot, the latter of whom tries to give an insight for the journalist into what his life was like when active as a drone pilot. The second narrative is spoken by a former drone pilot, 'Brandon', who explains the process by which a drone mission is carried out.

In the first interview, the journalist begins by asking: 'What's the difference between you and someone who sits in an aeroplane' to which the protagonist replies: 'There is no difference between us. We do the same job.' He goes on to refer to the fact that the principle of people being present within the zone of technological operation is becoming a historical idea. In this respect, the drone pilot, like the train operator or the aeroplane pilot, is indicative of skills that are now increasingly separated from the site of application.

The film is unsettling, not just because it describes the chaos of war, but also because it engages a form of war that is unfamiliar and which seems to operate by principles that are even more incoherent or inconsistent with our expectations of conflict than their current form. This is challenging because it makes additional demands on our moral conduct or requires us to be complicit in the moral distancing that another must undertake in order to act on our behalf. The absence of the drone pilot from the site of the conflict – from the site in which they would encounter risk, most adequately judge the implications of their destructive decisions, and where they put their own lives on the line in the course of such decision making – undermines an interpretation of war, and conflict more generally, which would want to ensure that acts of violence are undertaken with extreme consideration of their impact. Without being present within the site where destruction takes place, this may be lost.

In the film's second narrative, we encounter a story told by a former drone pilot. He states:

> *Five thousand feet is the best. We love it when we're sitting at five thousand feet. You have more description. Plus, at five thousand feet, I could tell you what type of shoes you're wearing. From a mile away!… So there are very clear cameras on-board. We have the 'IR', infrared, which we can switch to automatically. And that will pick up any heat signatures, or cold signatures. I mean, if someone sits down on a cold surface for a while and then gets up, you'll still see the heat from that person. For a long time. It kind of looks like a white blossom. Just shining up into heaven. It's quite beautiful.*

While military technology has always been on a trajectory that seeks the removal of the human from the site of highest risk, drones involve the complete removal of the human from the context of conflict and change the nature of what takes place when engaged in battle. While Boyle (2015) notes that this accusation of the drone weapon is misleading, as they are still heavily managed by human agents, they also acknowledge that the end game of such technology may involve such fully autonomous and non-human systems, machines versus machines.

Yet, there is also evidence that counters this characterisation of the drone military pilot. As the Task Force on Drone Policy (2015) notes, 'UAV operators are particularly vulnerable to post-traumatic stress: they may watch their targets for weeks or even months, seeing them go about the routines of daily life, before one day watching on-screen as they are obliterated' which may in fact lead to greater emotional and moral conflict, rather than less. Equally, Gregory (2011) notes that there may be even greater attachment to the context of conflict for drone pilots as they are also especially aware of the risks to their own troops, when undertaking strikes, which can reinforce the impact of actions. So, while drone operators are absent from the field of combat, a broader interpretation of this concept leads us to conclude that the presence is no less meaningful or consequential for them.

This is a view reiterated by Fast (2011), who, in defending the drone operator's attachment to the field of context, speaks of their experiencing a heightened awareness of their impact, perhaps even greater than that experienced by the soldier who is physically located in the field of combat (Kotz, 2012). Indeed, 'Brandon' states at one point in the interview that operating a drone is just like playing a video game, except for the fact that it cannot be switched off. Where drone operations are concerned, real lives are affected by every small decision that is made as a drone pilot and it is apparent that he feels great responsibility when undertaking such missions. This view is reinforced in the documentary film *National Bird*, which is structured around testimonies from three former US military drone operators turned whistle blowers. One of them, Heather Linebaugh (2013), explains her experience:

> *I may not have been on the ground in Afghanistan, but I watched parts of the conflict in great detail on a screen for days on end. I know the feeling you experience when you see someone die. Horrifying barely covers it. And when you are exposed to it over and over again it becomes like a small video, embedded in your head, forever on repeat, causing psychological pain and suffering that many people will hopefully never experience. UAV troops are*

> *victim to not only the haunting memories of this*
> *work that they carry with them, but also the guilt*
> *of always being a little unsure of how accurate*
> *their confirmations of weapons or identification of*
> *hostile individuals were.*

The implications of humans being absent from the field of combat are far wider than the degree to which personnel are morally engaged with their direct actions or whether they are psychologically affected in a way that is especially alarming. Moreover, Singer (2012) recognises that 'technologies that remove humans from the battlefield ... are becoming the new normal in war' (online) and that there has been nearly no debate about these changes to the act of war. For Singer, of most concern is that this change blurs the distinction between civilian and military roles. In this respect, Singer draws attention to the fact that there is also an absence of discussion by humans about such changes, which raises questions of control and responsibility.

The end game for drone-based warfare is rarely considered in military policy, a good example of which is found in the US Task Force on Drone Policy (2015). While recognising that drones render conventional legal terminologies fragile, the US policy does not consider the eventual consequence of a situation where, on both sides of a conflict, the human is removed from the field of combat. Instead, it reiterates the operating principle that, 'Since the dawn of mechanization, militaries have sought to replace people with more effective machines' (US Task Force on Drone Policy, 2015, p. 25).

However, it is the capacity to create simply more effective machines than one's adversary that secures military advantage. In a scenario where opposing powers have the same kinds of drones, they then cease to be effective as a means of securing dominance. A world in which all powers have their own powerful drones is a world that resembles that of a nuclear scenario, but where one can imagine an unending and persistent clashing of remote weapons, a perpetual battle fought out in space, concluded only when one set of machines fails to function.

MACHINES OUT OF CONTROL

These concerns have found renewed attention in an era of AI, where concerns about the future of humanity abound. Indeed, prominent public intellectuals with a history in taking on some of humanity's biggest challenges, such as Stephen Hawking have described AI as the biggest threat to humanity, with the potential to eradicate it completely (Cellen-Jones, 2014). These commentaries also apply to anxieties about drones, as one of the first pervasive AI machines within civil society today, with their capacity to move around by their own volition.

Such anxieties about humanity's redundancy and our being replaced by machines are evident across a long history of speculation about the future. For example, in 1770, Wolfgang von Kempelen constructed the now famous mechanical Turk, which may have been one of the world's first drones. The Turk was a 'fake chess-playing machine', which appeared as a mechanical robot capable of moving chess pieces on a board, seemingly making its own decisions. In actual fact, the machine was an illusion and, hidden inside, would have been a human chess master and an operator. Nevertheless, it was exhibited all over the world and is a remarkably early demonstration of the fascination with automation and the principles of drone technology, where a remote human makes decisions that are executed by a machine. In more recent times, we have seen how AI machines have demonstrated capacity to rival and even better humanity on a number of pursuits which we regard to represent the pinnacle of human cognitive capacity, such as playing chess. In this respect, the drone leads humanity to confront this imminent future, where its position as the supposedly omnipotent species on planet Earth is brought further into question.

From the moment that a drone flies up into the sky, humanity is confronted with the prospect of its redundancy and its being usurped by technology which takes control of Earth's future. Such themes have become common in discussions about robotics in recent years and have far reaching implications for how we think about humanity's place in the world and our society is organised as a result. For, unlike an aeroplane or helicopter, the drone flies off without us.

So significant is this absence of humanity and its replacement by a thinking machine that Singer (2012) describes its use as unconstitutional in the USA. He considers that military drones undermine democracy, by virtue of their short-circuiting 'the decision-making process for what used to be the most important choice a democracy could make' (Singer, 2012). Here, Singer is particularly concerned that drone weapons may be taking decisions to open fire on a target, without any human involvement. Yet, one might extend this to any number of applications, especially where human moral judgement is required. This is why discussions about drones are so crucial to human history, but also why they are so controversial. Drones are the first, highly sophisticated machines to occupy our social, physical world in a manner that hints at autonomous, mobile machines whose freedom of movement appears even to exceed that of humans.

As for the mechanical turk, or IBM's Deep Blue within the famous chess game against world chess master Gary Kasparov, we cannot see how the drone is thinking, nor make sense of what thinking means. We cannot identify the *ghost in the machine* and this may be deeply unsettling to humanity's sense of place within the world. Such machines depict a point in human history where technology is 'out of control' (Kelly, 1999) and this is especially troubling as they seem to have the capacity to invade our personal, social and physical space.

Drones may also undermine critical dimensions of humanity's distinct capacities, since they allow the species to undertake all kinds of atrocities without having to be physically connected or even cognitively engaged with the decision making around such actions. Furthermore, it is not simply through their deployment of weapons where one may identify the destructive contribution of drones. Undoubtedly, their capacity to bring destruction is central, but they are also used for such tasks as intelligence gathering and surveillance, refuelling, search and rescue, resupply, electronic attacks/jamming, psychological attacks, such as leaflet dropping, domestic border patrol and air combat (Gertler, 2012). Each of these functions is inextricable from an aspiration that is broadly destructive. The Task Force on US Drone Policy (2015) goes even further to reveal how the deployment of weapons is just one component of the destructive act. Thus, the military drone industry seeks to create a 'combat cloud', in which all automated vehicular interventions will exist. This reference to what is, in civilian terms, described as 'cloud computing', a term born out of the first dot com developers (Regalado, 2011), demonstrates how the internet of drones is quickly becoming a technological reality.

DRONE CRIMES AND LAW ENFORCEMENT

The crossover between military and civilian technologies is not unique to discussions about drone technology. For as long as theorists have interrogated the development of technology, there have been examples of how militaristic applications and patents have trickled down into civic life. Whether it is through the discovery of new materials or the invention of the automobile, the civilian use of technology is often a by-product of an initial, militaristic exploration and drones are no exception. While that relationship may be changing in a world where drone designs have become democratised, there is a cross-fertilisation between such commercial applications and other systems of surveillance and control.

An early example of such use is from February 2010, when the UK's Merseyside Police employed a drone to track a teenager who was fleeing from a car that was presumed to be stolen (Liverpool Echo, 2010). This quadrotor helicopter, named the 'hicam microdrone' weighed less than 1 kilogram, was less than 1 metre in diameter and was produced by German manufacturer GmBH (Page, 2010). Following the incident, the Merseyside police were placed under investigation for using a drone without approval from the UK's CAA and, subsequently, they suspended operations (Lewis, 2010). The case highlighted just how complicated it has been from the inception of the civilian drone era to ensure that operations take place lawfully. Since then, law enforcement officers around the world have used drones in countless settings, from general surveillance at high risk events to searching for missing people. In 2017, the UK's first drone policing unit was launched by Devon & Cornwall, aiming to equip all officers with a drone system to be used in emergency situations.

As for the military uses, the challenge for law enforcers is that the number of criminal uses of drones is also increasing. For example, drones have been used by criminals to transport goods to prisons (Ford, 2018). Alternatively, in 2018, criminal gangs were reported to have used drone swarms to intimidate and flush out FBI agents who were monitoring a hostage situation (Tucker, 2018). In 2017, the Trump administration began supporting plans to allow law enforcers to target and destroy drones on domestic soil, where they posed a threat (Savage, 2017) and these capacities were enshrined in the FAA Reauthorization Act of 2018 which 'gives freedom from law enforcement bodies to use reasonable force, if necessary, to disable, damage, or destroy the unmanned aircraft system or unmanned Aircraft' (U.S. Government, 2018).

The need for the police to utilise drones as a means of control is mirrored by the use of drones to commit crimes. Here, among the most prominent stories are those that involve pilots flying drones to disrupt social events or political gatherings, often through unlawful flying. For example in October 2014, during a Euro 2016 qualifying football match between Serbia and Albania, a drone was flown over the playing field with an Albanian nationalist flag dangling below it, as a political statement about the relationship between these two nations. The flag was flown close to the players, which quickly led to violence on the playing field, involving fans and players, causing the game to be abandoned. While the pilot explained later his intention was to deliver the flag to the Albanian half of the pitch, a misunderstanding of the team colours, led him to land the flag among the opposition (Montague, 2015).

CONCLUSION: WHEN IS BAD GOOD?

Determining the moral content of any single drone application is no easy task, in part, because very few of the actions undertaken by law keepers or outlaws operate in isolation of each other. For example, is a drone delivery platform used for transporting illegal drugs to people a morally worse situation than compared with such drugs being transported by people directly on their person? The challenge accompanying these examples is that, in order for them to be effective, they must also be harder to detect by the authorities. In this sense, these bad applications have even worse consequences for the authorities, who are seeking to avoid a situation where these products are able to arrive at their destination without interruption. If drones mean that authorities are more likely to fail to keep prisons free from contraband, then this seems certainly to be a bad consequence of the drone revolution.

One may argue that technology is value neutral and that it is only in the application that one can determine its moral content. Yet, this analysis would seem to apply mostly to experimental design work, rather than the examples mentioned here. The creation of the Predator drone is not simply value neutral, even if it occupies a world in which there are contested debates about whether weapon development is principally a function of the desire to defend and protect versus the desire to impose a way of life on another nation by force. The problem with the defence proposition is that it then permits any weapon to be justified on the basis of defence, which is clearly contrary to the intuitive and evidential impact of weapon designs, which is that they are used to assert ideological will upon a population or individual.

This is worrisome when taking into account the degree to which military applications may also inform efforts to make civilian policing more effective. Indeed, Jenson (2016) describes how military operations must be understood as intimately connected to efficiencies made within civilian policing, perhaps even to a point where it makes little sense to distinguish between spaces that are foreign to a nation and thus determined as zones of conflict, and domestic, geographic territories. This is especially true in a climate where the so-called war on terror permits authorities to treat domestic territory as part of the battlefield, in need of continuous surveillance to ensure that swift responses are possible. What seems clear within these debates about the future of conflict, is that drones will have a big part to play going forward.

5

THE BEAUTIFUL

While drones may be regarded as mostly functional platforms – tools designed with a mission or task in mind – one of the most surprising areas of drone applications is found within creative and artistic exploration. This is not to say that artistic practice lacks function or even utility. Indeed, it is widely acknowledged that creative practice plays a central role to a nation's economic vitality, along with making an even more important contribution to knowledge. Rather, it is to recognise that the principal value one may derive from such endeavours has nothing to do with the achievement of some goal, other than the pursuit of some creative expression.

For nearly 10 years, choreographers, photographers, filmmakers, musicians and performers have each employed drones to explore their creative ambitions, in a way that speaks to a much wider history of artistic innovation that can be traced across the centuries. In this sense, drones are no different from any other new, creative medium, whether it is paint, light, video, photography or even artificial intelligence. Drones have rapidly become the next new medium for artists to play with and create artistic experiences that have hitherto been impossible to achieve.

By critically discussing how artistic drone creations have shaped and responded to the meaning and values people attach to drones, this chapter considers the distinctiveness of these pursuits. More broadly, it examines the relationship between art, science and engineering, which are reified by drone art. It will show how creative propositions that involve drones have often taken on the greatest engineering challenges and how this has forged new collaborations between researchers, technologists and creatives. By examining such work, one may derive greater insights into the common ground between art and science, but also better understand what kind of world emerges by pursuing a future in which drones occupy the space around us. To this end, this chapter outlines how drone artists have engaged with a number of critical concerns over humanity's future, not least of which is over the limits to which technology may be put.

The subject of beauty foregrounds these discussions, not because all art must be beautiful, but because an interest in aesthetics is present within many of the artistic endeavours discussed here. Indeed, the aspiration to create something beautiful with drones has occupied the interests of artists as much as the desire to create art that confronts the societal concerns associated with drones. While each will be discussed at length, the focus on aesthetics rather than function is the central thread within this chapter, which begins by examining the relationship between art, science and engineering, and how drones challenge our assumptions about their differences and separation.

While modern societies mostly distinguish art and science as distinct modes of inquiry, particularly in the institutional education setting, this chapter examines drone art to reveal why it is crucial that these two worlds are brought closer together. It also examines the historical development of artistic drone creations, discussing their importance as manifestations of tensions in humanity's utilisation of technology. From criticisms on global political conflicts and humanity's attempts to resolve them through military interventions, to the use of drones as tools of artistic activism and cultural criticism, to the emergence of entirely new creative practices, this chapter puts into context the importance of efforts to democratise the drone. In doing so, it examines how such attempts have involved subjecting the drone to a range of human interests, to realise their potential and to ensure that any loss to humanity arising from autonomous machines is minimised and far exceeded by the gains afforded by these new technologies.

BRIDGING ART, SCIENCE AND ENGINEERING

Despite their often being separated within societal systems, one of the principal ways in which scientific and artistic inquiries similar is through the development of new techniques of investigation. After all, all knowledge-based insights arise through the creation of methodologies which seek to permit greater access to the world's mysteries and, in this respect, what takes place within art is not so very different from what takes place within scientific inquiry. In terms of technology, the point at which these two worlds come together is often through the process of invention.

Consider the first time that somebody articulated the design of a functional flying vehicle: a balloon, a plane or even a drone. These were all moments of extraordinarily creative innovation involving the act of imagining something that had previously been unexpressed in recorded history. As Van Riper (2004) notes, the first ideas about humans developing 'powered flight' (p. 12) could be found in 'novels, short stories, poetry, paintings, cartoons, and scores of magazine articles'. Indeed, if one wants to understand what the future looks like, then one would do well to explore such literature, before even turning to present day scientific discoveries or achievements in engineering that may be expressed within the scholarly journals.

It is no coincidence then, that science often has its roots in science fiction, despite the unease of many scientists to recognise such foundations. Expression within science fiction of some future world, which may later be revealed by science as achievable, is where one can discover many initial efforts in design. Consider the Babelfish in Douglas Adams' *The Hitchhiker's Guide to the Galaxy*, which is an alien life form capable of performing instant translations into any language by sliding into the user's ear. Years later, technologists have created a series of real-world devices that emulate this facility, including Microsoft Skype's real-time translation software, which launched as a beta product in 2015 (Pavulus, 2015), and Google's Translate function, launched in May 2019 under the wonderfully futuristic name, the *Translatotron*. Although it requires a degree of creative imagination to join these two histories together, their occurring via separate trajectories does not undermine the claim that scientific research and technology designs often have their origins within fiction.

Moreover, provocations about the future arising from 'design fiction' (Bleeker, 2009; Sterling, 2005) are central to the proliferation of technologies within our society. In this respect, drones are no exception. Indeed, the initial manifestation of drone applications can be traced through the prototypes mentioned earlier and the patent applications, as works of fiction, but they also are found within highly sophisticated storytelling platforms, such as science fiction literature or film.

Without having first imagined the quadcopter within some design fiction, there would be no opportunity to find function within its creation. Yet, even here, to determine the origins of a drone's design, one must traverse a range of technologies.

For example, while Oehmichen originated the quadcopter design in 1920, he also pioneered the achievement of helicopter designs. Even then, his quadcopter may be highly separated from the twenty-first century micro-quadcopters, though it exists as a reference point for establishing principles in aviation that go beyond those early achievements in aviation. Back then, the fiction of those times was to imagine the kinds of capabilities that are now achieved through modern technology, but the importance of imagining those possibilities is crucial to the design process.

In sum, without artistic imagination, there would be no technological society, no scientific discoveries and no capacity to imagine the world differently. Each of these endeavours is located within the broader pursuit of creation, whether that is the creation of new theories, ideas, insights or artefacts. Moreover, artistic practice helps us to interpret the world through a multitude of lenses, which may not be available to us were it not for such inquiries. The singular act of invention – as a manifestation of such inquiries – engages our imagination in ways that are similar to the manner in which artists work. Indeed, scientists have often utilised artistic techniques to develop scientific appraisals of the world. Whether it is Watson, Crick and Franklin's characterisation of DNA as a double helix, or Darwin's reliance on illustrating the species he discovered, artistic practice is present throughout the history of science. Indeed, humanity's entire understanding of prehistoric life is reliant on artistic interpretation. In engineering, this is equally profound, as the creation of structures, from bridges to buildings and even nanomolecular scale scaffolds relies on the ability to function creatively. And this is particularly true of drone art.

Consider the 2019 realisation of a drone firework display produced by a creative team at Intel. In this case, the creative team's achievement is inextricable from a series of other drone displays that had been created in the context of large scale, high-profile events, such as the Olympic Games in 2018. Indeed, Intel's work in drone choreographies has been present at a number of major events around the world since 2016. At the PyeongChang 2018 Olympic Games, their display of 1218 drones flying together to create three-dimensional shapes of athletes and even the Olympic rings, broke the world record for drone choreography.

Intel's subsequent drone fireworks display was their team's next iteration, demonstrating even greater capability and imagination. The drones took off, and then lit up the sky using on-board super-bright LEDs, their lighting sequence emulating the light patterns we see when fireworks appear in the sky. As the audience sat in the darkness watching the drone fireworks performance, the drones appeared as three-dimensional sky sculptures, connected to each other through data and software, emulating the light display and patterns of fireworks. While the performance was, again, a world-record breaking achievement in engineering, it was also a unique moment of artistic insight and accomplishment and evidence of how artistic practice evolves alongside technology. Yet, beyond just being a remarkable technological feat, the achievement of a drone firework display calls into question the value of its previous form, the traditional firework, itself born out of a particular knowledge of how to mix chemicals in a way that can create such vehicles of audio-visual spectacles dating back hundreds of years. Writing of their work, Intel VP Anil Nanduri describes how drone firework shows are 'modern-day fireworks that are green, reusable and more precise, providing programmable control for a new generation of aerial artisans and technicians.' (Nanduri, 2018).

Thus, in a world where drones can create wonderful light displays on a large scale, there may be more value in utilising them, rather than conventional fireworks. While Chinese firework artist Cai Guo-Qiang may contest this, the claim speaks more to how new technology gives rise to new forms of artistic creation which are, nevertheless, situated in a history of other creative practices. Intel's drone fireworks are able to do more than just emulate the aerial spectacle of fireworks; they are able to also reorganise themselves into many other three-dimensional shapes. This model is now expanding, as the technology proliferates, with Walt Disney submitting a patent application for 'Flixel's – their firework drone proposal – in 2015, which would replace their daily fireworks show. This aspiration was accompanied by a petition from Walt Disney to the FAA for an exemption to the rules on flight restrictions (Walt Disney, 2015), which was subsequently approved (FAA, 2016).

One of the distinguishing characteristics of such artistic work is the relationship between the material reality of drones, flying in geographical space and the successful modelling of their behaviours within a data cloud located within software. On one level, drone choreographies are like painting by numbers in three dimensions; the flight paths are all mapped out in data before any drone takes off and their coordination is all automated. Indeed, one might easily watch the animated data model which underpins the physical world manifestation and regard that as an artistic work in its own right. The manifestation of this data within a physical choreography is a surrogate to the data configuration. If one really wants to appreciate the artwork, then it is necessary to make sense of the code's complexity, which itself may be awe inspiring. Yet, it is the drone's occupation of space – or, indeed, of space that looks down upon humans – where one finds the most compelling narrative of drone art, as evidencing the machine's omnipotence. The firework drones display is a physical manifestation of data; a series of models that are, first, constructed digitally, before rendering them in the real world. In this sense, they are more akin to forms of architecture than of any other artistic form.

Yet, the connection between drone technologies and artistic practice run even deeper than this. Indeed, identifying the earliest examples of drone art is not easy, in part because the idea of a drone is symbolically present in many other concepts, which have deep roots in human history, made evident in artistic practice through the ages. For example, ideas within religious texts may be assembled into forms that are present within our analyses of what is at stake with the emergence of autonomous drones. Thus, the notion that there exists a high authority – a God-like entity – which is, in some way, overseeing the playing out of human actions – rather like how we may be creating autonomous machines – or who may have some overarching plan for humanity, is a persistent and deeply ingrained feature of human history.

In this sense, drones engages us with the idea that the human use of technology ushers in a new, potentially, disruptive force in some notion of a natural order. In this sense, one may refer to artwork that describes stories of religious texts as manifestations of early drone art. Indeed, one of the earliest renowned artistic accomplishments with drones was produced by the creative technology collective Marshmallow Laser Feast (MLF). In 2012, MLF's inaugural drone performance was the opening show in the Saatchi and Saatchi New Directors' showcase, the theme of which was titled 'Meet Your Creator'. Their kinetic sculpture, set upon a theatre stage, involved 16 drones 'dancing in a joyous robo-ballet celebration of techno-spirituality' (Memo, 2012) to music by Oneohtrix Point Never, an experimental electronic music composer. The drones were adorned with lights and mirrors, the latter of which reflected light projected at them from tracker spot lights. Speaking of the MLF presentation, Memo Atken describes how:

> *The theme of the event, is 'Meet your creator',*
> *referring to the directors in the reel obviously, but*
> *it implies a cheeky double meaning, a religious*
> *connotation of meeting your 'Creator'. After many*
> *brainstorms, this idea evolved to position the event*
> *as a congregation, and the whole audience, disciples*
> *of an imaginary religion that values and cherishes*
> *creativity, creation. It is a religion where we are all*
> *creators, and are driven by the urge to create, and*
> *appreciate other people's creations. We wanted to*
> *attach a level of appreciation to this analogous to*
> *that of a trance inducing evangelical worship. (2012)*

Elsewhere, Atken writes of MLF's desire to re-interpret the drone through artistic work, in the wake of a tidal wave of public discourse on the drone's destructive behaviour as weapons of war. In this respect, MLF's pioneering performance at the Saatchi showcase reveals how, often, artistic contributions to imagining the drone have been conceived as responses to or commentaries on their immediate political occupation, as artefacts of war. The work also draws attention to the unpredictability of technological systems, as the performance does not precisely emulate the predicted movements, instead interpreting data and presenting it back to the audience without complete human control.

While the idea of drones occupying the space of creator, rather like the literary notion of a divine creator, our analysis will not take us much further in this direction, as there is much in recent drone art history to occupy our attention. Nevertheless, it is significant to recognise that the modern day drone artist and the cultural meanings of the drone need interpreting along such lines, and it is perhaps only art that permits such discoveries.

DRONES AS ARTISTIC ACTIVISM

Although MLF sought to re-interpret the drone and explore the possibility of undermining its destructive persona by giving it an almost omnipotent creative identity, other artists have sought to engage with the political history of drones by direct and explicit references of such behaviours within their artwork. Notably, James Bridle's 'Under the Shadow of the Drone' (2012) and 'Dronestagram' describes a series of works dating from 2012 to 2015, which engage us with the idea that drones are all around us, infiltrating our lives, even if we do not see them.

In the case of the drone shadows, Bridle's work consist of single-line drawings depicting what he describes as the 'canonical' drone – the shape of the US Predator drone – an image which became popularised as the destructive machines used in military missions. Bridle would use white tape laid out on the ground in a public space to create a life-size outline of the drone's shape. The outline resembles the classical manner in which police would outline a dead body at a crime scene with chalk, to provide the trace of the person after the body has been removed.

In doing so, Bridle's art directly confronts the political activities of predatory drones – and the US Predator drone in particular – speaking to the blurred territory of art and activism. His work draws attention to how drones inhabit the spaces in which people live, even if they do not notice them. These vehicles pass by our homes on their way to commit some destructive act. Yet, of most concern to Bridle is the moral implications of drones, which his work seeks to articulate. He states:

> *We all live under the shadow of the drone, although*
> *most of us are lucky enough not to live under its*
> *direct fire. But the attitude they represent – of*
> *technology used for obscuration and violence; of*
> *the obfuscation of morality and culpability; of*
> *the illusion of omniscience and omnipotence; of*
> *the lesser value of other people's lives; of, frankly,*
> *endless war – should concern us all. (Bridle, 2012)*

Bridle's work also enquires into how one may understand the drone as a new node within our digital society. In this respect, his Shadows also alert us to the idea that the network is not just all around us, it is also mobile, and capable of moving across space and time, infiltrating areas of the world that we may previously have thought to be out of the bounds of our digital lives. In this respect, the drone represents the network becoming a living entity, transcending its otherwise immobile structures, tied to large data servers that are reliant on cables and satellites. In part, this is what makes the drone such a phenomenal technology, as it allows a radical detachment of the technology from a physical infrastructure.

For Bridle, the drone is also deeply intertwined with our imagination about the future of technology. The drone that Bridle uses to create the outlines is, itself, based on a highly popularised image of the Predator drone, which was a computer-generated composite image, created by an amateur enthusiast, rather than a photograph of the actual Predator. In this sense, the public's imagination about drones was informed by what was essentially an artistic interpretation, albeit one that bore close relation to the reality.

Bridle also describes his artistic contribution as a commentary on the invisible and intangible qualities of technology today. The drone flies at 50,000 feet, which is too far for people on the ground to see. Moreover, like much of today's technology, the drone is also beyond most people's comprehension or capacity to understand technically. In this sense, it appears as a kind of magical force or, again, some form of presence that is beyond the physical world, seemingly supernatural in its gravity defying abilities.

Importantly, Bridle's work is accompanied by his *Drone Shadows Handbook*, which outlines how to replicate his work. The Handbook has enabled others to create their own instantiations of the drone shadow, thus functioning as artefacts of political protest, commentary and community. Bridle notes that drone shadows have been drawn at the site of arms fairs and even next to the USA Whitehouse, as a protest against the use of drones as weapons (Bridle, 2015).

Finally, as a complement to Drone Shadows work, Bridle's *Dronestagram* series consists of posting photographs of 'the landscapes of drone strikes to Instagram'. Through this work, Bridle interrogates the dissonance between the predominance of social media as a space that lays claim to be an all-encompassing manifestation of modern lives and the fact that it is rarely the horrors of the world that we share through such platforms. He states:

> *if these social media are supposed, as all the marketing speak says, to bring us all closer together, to provide a glimpse of each others' daily realities, shouldn't we use them to see a little bit further? (Bridle, 2014)*

Other artistic contributions with drones have focussed on matters of global injustice. For example, *Unequal Scenes* by Johnny Miller illustrates matters of political concern by employing drones to create photographs that reveal the world to us in ways we may not see so readily. In this case,

Miller exposes the inequalities that exist within our world, but which can only be seen from the drone's unique vantage point (Miller, 2017). Each image adopts a perspective that reveals the close geographic relationship between communities of dramatically varied economic means. For instance, one photograph from Mumbai shows how 'Billion-dollar houses in the form of skyscrapers exist next to vast slums covered in blue tarps against the monsoon rains' (Miller, 2017).

In this case, the drone's perspective on the world sheds new light on our appreciation for the existence of inequalities – they are irrefutable evidence of the significant divisions between rich and poor that exist within our societies. In this sense, the work causes us to reflect also on the quote from the former drone pilot in the movie *5,000 Feet is the Best* – who states that, at this height, the degree of detail on the world is so great, that the drone's camera can see the colour of someone's hair or the kind of shoes they are wearing. Upon seeing Miller's images, one can imagine that the artist aspires for the viewer to be more engaged with the inequalities that surround them and, perhaps, for that to inspire some kind of social change.

Another prominent example is IOCOSE's *drone selfies* (2014), which form part of their wider project *In Times of Peace*, a series which 'explores the life of a drone after war and terror'. The selfies consist of photographs taken from a drone's on-board camera while it is hovering in front of a mirror. The result of their photography is a selfie – a photographic self-portrait – absent of any human, but situated within a very human, everyday setting. This series of images imbues the drone with a sense of agency and autonomy and involves their undertaking actions that have become symbolic of humanity's obsession with locating the constructed image of the self at the heart of public life.

As it undertakes a practice that has hitherto been the sole preserve of humans to date, IOCOSE draw our attention to an impending era of fully autonomous flying robots, asking us what kinds of things they might do. Yet, it also engages viewers with the complexity of the unreal. In the same way that the human selfie is a reconstructed, idealised version of ourselves – with the filters and body modifications that are made possible by mobile camera technology – the drone emulates the desire to see itself differently, not as an object of destruction, but as a personality of worth in its own right, irrespective of its past deeds. The images ask the viewer to think about their place in the world and what they are asking technology to do on their behalf. It also invites consideration of the impact of creating artificially intelligent machines and the possibility that they may, one day, develop their own self-interest and self-awareness.

A final, important contribution to drone art is found in the work of the artist collective, *Team Black Sheep*, which has sought to interrogate the regulation of civilian air space. Their drone films from prominent urban centres such as New York and London express the discontinuity between the regulatory debates that focus on the safety of the general public, and the apparent fun and enjoyment shared by those whom they have captured on film. Team Black Sheep's founder, Raphael 'Trappy' Pirker, also articulates the manner in which drones occupy multiple terrains as forms of art work, investigation, education and provocation. He notes 'we try to demonstrate that the current law [governing drone use] is not really helping anybody' (Pirker, cited in Holland, 2013). The challenge confronting such work is to answer how the public interest is served when the public is put at risk as a result of such activism.

DRONES AS CRITICAL DESIGN WORK

While there is an obvious political interpretation that follows from how artists have responded to the militaristic uses of drones, there are also artistic contributions that speak to wider aspects of cultural change. Through artistic practice, these concerns – or aspirations – for the drone are found within their characterisation of what Dunne and Raby (2014) describe as 'critical design'. Such investigations inform us of key social, cultural and political issues that drones present for us, while also identify wider social critiques that the drones may permit in ways that are otherwise unachievable.

One of the most prominent drone artists whose designs have been used to make art is KATSU, who created a drone capable of spraying graffiti. To appreciate the importance of this work, one first needs to consider what is the social function of graffiti and there are at least two ways to interpret such work. On one level, one may treat graffiti as simply a form of vandalism, which legally is a reasonable position to hold. However, a deeper reading of why such vandalism arises may have something to do with the manner in which space, buildings, and objects are managed as private systems of governance and restriction.

In this sense, the graffiti artist, by tagging their name, or creating even more elaborate work, seeks to assert themselves within such a context, to disrupt or undermine the ownership economy. Indeed, one may describe why there is often an association between other practices, such as skateboarding, which simply involves reclaiming public space for alternative purposes. In this sense, the graffiti artist rejects the ownership and restrictions placed upon citizens and reclaims space for themselves. This is especially true in spaces that are hard to reach and some of the most notable graffiti artists have value for this reason especially. For example, the Banksy murals at the wall separating Gaza and Israel perform both a deep political commentary, while also evidence the re-occupation of space that has been purposely designed to separate populations who are in conflict.

In the case of KATSU, the most widely discussed intervention involved flying a drone in New York and defacing a Calvin Klein billboard, which was treated as a criticism of consumerism, celebrity and media culture. As Boucher (2015) describes:

> *Even if you're not a fan of graffiti, maybe you can get behind vandalism as a way of defacing the most visible instances of capitalism's intrusion into the visual landscape, especially when they traffic in unrealistic standards of beauty. A previous billboard at the same location featured a topless Justin Bieber that digitally enhanced both his muscles and his manhood.*

Importantly, KATSU discusses the defacement of the billboard not simply as vandalism, but as a painting in its own right. The wider artistic work of KATSU in exploring AI-based drone paintings – which he calls 'Dronescapes' – is also an inquiry into the potential of machines to create their own art work – and of humanity's willingness to recognise such activity as art. In this sense, KATSU's work is also an investigation into the future of humanity and the prospect of a world in which autonomous machines live among us, performing functions and even making art work. Such ideas also taken up in MNEMODRONE, an artistic project devised as a commentary on a future in which humans will co-exist with artificially intelligent beings.

KATSU's work also encourages its viewer to reflect on how other artistic practices may develop alongside digital societies, particularly the capitalist context of the digital economy. For instance, his earlier work explored the idea of creating graffiti tags within computer games – Minecraft being among the first. As more of our public lives become located less in physical space and more in digital space, digital surfaces are an entirely appropriate, new context for the graffiti artist.

In this sense, one may treat graffiti as a kind of physical space hacking, as we might talk also of digital hacking. A further interesting facet to KATSU's graffiti drone is that the design specifications are made available to other artists as Open Source coding. In a way similar to James Bridle's Handbook for Drone Shadows, KATSU seeks to democratise the process of creating art through technology, which may be seen also as a critique on the, otherwise, proprietary culture that surrounds innovation. KATSU even encourages other artists to paint over his art work and reclaim the space for their own. A further central thread within this work draws on Mumford's (1934/2010) notion that the value neutral nature of technology is undermined by its being situated within capitalist systems. He states:

> *It was because of certain traits in private capitalism that the machine – which was a neutral agent – has often seemed a malicious element in society, careless of human life, indifferent to human interests. The machine has suffered for the sins of capitalism; contrariwise, capitalism has often taken credit for the virtues of the machine. (pp. 27–28)*

If only humanity can break from such logic, then – as KATSU's wider work conveys – it may be possible to more adequately realise the positive potential of technology.

DRONE PERFORMERS

Early on in their recent history, drones have also been utilised in theatre as props or performers, where key contributions have been made by Spaxels, Liam Young and Marshmallow Laser Feast, mentioned earlier. In Young's case, his major contributions took a range of forms, notably in his creation of 'couture drones'. These drones took a reasonably standard quadrotor drone, which were then adorned with various costumes, creating their own sense of fashionable wear. In doing so, Young pushes back against the idea that drones – much like many other technologies – are absent of any distinguishing, personalising features.

In today's technological world, objects are all designed to be similar, the economies of scale that operate around them function most efficiently in this way. Mobile phones, televisions, cars, all arrive to us indistinguishable from any other that rolls off the production line. They are devoid of character and identity and we try to imbue them with unique characters by personalising them. Young's drones inhabit distinct personalities and their presence hints at a future where robots may be imbued deliberately with varied personalities, to ensure they are more easily relatable to humans. Their most notable performance took place in London in 2014, as part of a performance with drone music legend John Cale and his band in a performance.

One of the most prominent early examples of performing drones is found in the co-production of SPARKED (Cirque du Soleil, 2014), which brought together drone specialist Raffaelo D'Andrea and the world-renowned theatrical company Cirque du Soleil. Described as a 'live interaction between humans and quadcopters' SPARKED is a short narrative film, which is set within an imagined electrician's workshop. It begins with the protagonist tinkering away with electrical devices, surrounded by lamps, awaiting repair.

As the film progresses, the lights gradually go out, prompting the tired worker to resort to a gas lamp until, suddenly, the lampshades spark to life. Gradually, the lampshades fly off the table and into the workroom, surrounding the electrician, who is filled with wonder, gradually noticing that the lampshades are responding to his own gestures. As he moves his arms, the lampshades – obscuring drones beneath them – move with his gestures. The film engages us with ideas of autonomous objects and magic, but crucially demonstrate an actual engineering achievement realised by D'Andrea – gesture-controlled drones. This feat of engineering is demonstrated in a widely watched TED video, showing D'Andrea interacting with a drone through arm gestures and, since, a number of drones have been realised with this kind of feature.

DRONE CHOREOGRAPHIES

As mentioned earlier, Intel's firework choreographies are among the most accomplished drone choreographies, but others exist, evidencing even further the interrelations among artists, scientists and engineers. Notably, a ground-breaking artistic contribution with swarming drones was made by the Ars Electronica FutureLab programme, which gave rise to Spaxels, an initiative that sought to explore the creative potential of swarm-based drone technology. The term Spaxels evokes the notion of a pixel located in three-dimensional physical space, with the two words of space and pixel combining to describe a new form of data-driven aerial choreography using drones. Among their many accomplishments are the creation of the Star Trek insignia over London, an event which marked Earth Hour in 2013, coinciding with the launch of the new Star Trek in Darkness movie. The Ars Electronica group worked closely with Intel in the development of choreographies, perhaps the most significant accomplishment was their world-record breaking 'Drone 100' performance in 2015, which was revealed as a keynote at CES in Las Vegas in 2016 (Swatman, 2016).

The notable similarity between, Intel, Spaxels and MLF is their creation of swarm-based drone performances. Indeed, the engineering challenge of ensuring drones that can fly alongside each other in predictable ways has occupied the attention of many drone developers, which provide insights into the collaboration that takes place between world-leading engineer teams and artistic groups. Indeed, swarm drone systems have attracted the interest of scientists and the military. For example, Lipinski and Mohseni (2016) explore the potential of a drone swarm to enter the space of a hurricane, as it happens and monitor what is happening from within. Such applications may be able to provide real-time monitoring to ascertain the development of a hurricane and assess potential risks.

Unifying these performing drones is a degree of ambiguity over how we may regard their contribution within art history. Do we refer to these works as props, actor, dancers or some other idea that we have yet to invent? Often, their role within shows is multifaceted – their physical presence creates a sculptured presence within a stage – even constituting the parameters of the stage. Elsewhere, they may also combine being hosts to other objects, as in the case of the *Eleven Play* dance performance (Rosenthal, 2014). In this case, three drones dance together alongside three human dancers, but they are also carrying lighting equipment, so as to illuminate the human subject. In this manner, it may be correct to characterise the drones as being in the service of the human, but the attention given to the drones by the dancers and their prominence within the stage means that all eyes are focussed on what the drones are doing.

DRONES FOR FILMMAKING

As mentioned in Chapter 2, one of the most popular applications of drones today is their use as filmmaking platforms. The capacity to capture the world from a perspective that humans can otherwise not reach has led to many hobbyists developing new skills in filmmaking. Beyond amateur filmmaking, the practice of drone filmmaking has led to considerable experimentation within professional filmmaking, which has advanced the artistic practice in fascinating ways. Notably, Liam Young's work has progressed into experimental filmmaking propositions where drones occupy various roles within the film. As a filmmaker, Young works on iterative works of art, which are presented as versions of a developmental vision. However, his always unfinished style to film making cannot be characterised as guerrilla art, but as a highly developed cinematic rendering of our everyday world, drawing attention to the centrality of technology in establishing our sense of a social reality. As part of a three film series, *In the Robot Skies* (Young, 2016) sees Young create the first narrative film constructed entirely of drone footage.

Young's work develops in a time when drone filmmaking has become its own art form. In 2015, the world's first drone film festival took place in New York, with a number of others popping up around the world in the following years. By its second year, there were a number of ways in which the creative community were beginning to define this new kind of filmmaking. For instance, the categories of film in 2016 were: extreme sports & best in show, technical, featuring drones, narrative, news & documentary, architecture, dronie, landscape, audience choice award, freestyle FPV, x-factor, showreel and still photography. It is not often that the beginnings of an art form mature so publicly, and far less often to see it documented in a way that has been possible with drone filmmaking.

Since then, drone filmmakers have become sought-after experts, as budgets for films and, indeed, certain kinds of aerial cinematography have been made possible only by the drone. It thus has developed a personality of its own and filmmakers have sought to utilise the drone to tell new stories of familiar places. A good example of this is the BBC's drone film of the Auschwitz concentration camp site, which they released in January 2015 – 100 year anniversary of World War 1 (BBC, 2015). The film shows a drone flying throughout the remains of the concentration camp, beginning at a low-level altitude and steadily rising to give an overview of the enormity of the place. The film signalled an era of how drone footage would become a central feature of journalism and documentary.

The creation of the New York City Drone Film Festival also marked a new form of professional filmmaking, which has implications beyond just capturing our lives and turning them into personal albums. For professional filmmakers, drones permit the exploration of a new art form, a new kind of filmmaking, which may operate by a very different creative language. Some films from the festival stand alone as pieces shot entirely by a drone, without much other technical dimensions. For example, *Floater* (Fischer, 2016) begins with an overhead shot of a man floating in the ocean, his body filling the frame. The remainder of the film is simply a slow zoom back, as the drone ascends, eventually showing just how isolated the swimmer is from anything else. He is seemingly miles from anywhere, simply floating in the water, relaxed, unconcerned and at peace. The film achieves what many drone films aspire to convey, which is a sense of epic proportions, depicting such wide perspectives on an area, so as to inspire a sense of awe.

The art of drone filmmaking is still emerging, but practitioners have already developed principles of operation which draw out specific kinds of aesthetic values around different forms of drone film. In the NYCDFF community, practitioners write about tips for filmmakers, ranging from technical details about camera operations to specifying flight modes for different kinds of film. For example, experts write about using the auto-levelling mode when filming, to create a more stable shot, or using the highest resolution possible at 4:3 ratio to obtain the widest picture. There is also considerable work undertaken in post-production to create some of the smoothest lines that are seen in many drone films. While the skills of drone filmmaking art still emerging, these films and the ideas of the leading practitioners articulate the emergence of a new art form in cinematography, which is extending the creative potential of film, while also creating an entirely new set of expectations from the medium.

CONCLUSION

Despite the opportunities afforded by drone art to realise new forms of creative expression, these examples are not without controversy among art circles. For instance, work by KATSU is written about as having the potential 'to transform graffiti forever' (Michel, 2015) and not necessarily for the better. After all, one of the central features of the enigma of graffiti is the fact that it appears in places that are difficult for people to reach. This may be due to the location being within a space that is regulated or governed, such as a building or a train, or might be due to the fact that the places are physically hard to access, or it might be due to both.

On one level, graffiti in hard to reach places signifies humanity's capacity to undermine such restrictions on our freedom to roam and the legitimacy of the inaccessible, built up world, which keeps people down on the ground, outside of the realms of large skyscrapers. As such, the presence of the artist within the space is central to that social value. Yet, remotely piloted drones remove the artist from the location unless, of course, they undertake the work within places that are impossible to access by any other means. They no longer need to find ways of being present within the space and something may be lost in the art of graffiti as a result of this displacement. As well, the technological dependency of the drone artist means their work is often inherently collaborative, making it harder to locate the artist within the creation. In one respect, the most creative contributor in drone choreography may be the team of coders who create the programming to arrange the drones and ensure they can fly alongside each other in synchronicity, rather than the artist. Yet, certainly, in each of these matters, there are rich discussions to be had in establishing what distinguishes art in the twenty-first century and how it may be evolving alongside technology to create even more radical ways of imagining the future.

Conclusion

DRONES FOR GOOD?

Drones are objects imbued with a range of historic imaginations about humanity's future. They symbolise humanity's transition from a point in time where they exist among machines that are largely under their control, to a situation where machines have the intellectual capacity and physical mobility that exceeds humanity's own and where control is in question. This is not to say that the drone symbolises humanity's demise or its being overrun by machines. Rather, it is to recognise that the drone compels us to think about the direction in which technology is taking humanity and more adequately frame the prospect of a computational singularity not only just in terms of computer power, but also in terms of mobility. The drone gives a physical presence to the prospect of the singularity and, as a result, more adequately constitutes a disruptive invasion of human space and society.

The pace of change within drone technology, humanity's trepidation into this world as evidenced by the lag between regulation and use, and the polarisation of views that drones provoke among people, are wonderfully compelling ingredients for a debate that is only just beginning.

When *Project Daedalus* began its life in 2013, humanity was on the cusp of a civilian drone expansion. As it progressed, our team was mesmerised by the relentless innovation that took place in a remarkably short space of time. Barely a week went by without some new drone design being launched into the world, or a new application being realised, or a new form of disruption occurring via a drone. What began as a project to explore the creative potential of drones led to further inter-rogations over society's readiness for their proliferation.

Since then, new forms of human behaviour have emerged around the utilisation of drones, which is reminiscent of the manner in which other big technological shifts changed humanity; like bicycles or the internet, drones reveal how our world may be organised differently. Drones have become platforms through which technological innovation in a num-ber of sectors have found application and where a new gen-eration of robotics is being realised.

UNCERTAIN FUTURES

There remain questions over whether the 'Drones for Good' applications will adequately demonstrate value to such a degree that we can expect drones to continually prolifer-ate across our physical world, or whether their applications will become even more frustrated by the complexities of our social configurations. Still, drones are pioneering technologies in the coming age of intelligent machines, representing our growing proximity to the technological singularity, and the age of connecting things, which not only have a data-based intelligence, but which can also undertake actions in the phys-ical world that reconfigure it in crucial ways. Unlike the com-puter, the car or the spaceship, the drone makes manifest the implications of machines being able to determine their own fate, without humanity's influence. As such, drones are far more profound than any other machine in our history and are often treated in ways that epitomise anxieties about humanity's future.

One indication of these radical changes was evidenced in how the UK's CAA discussed the technological trends surrounding drone platforms. In its 6th Guidelines for UAV from 2015, it outlined a number of future policy concerns. Together, these concerns, expressed by the principal regulator of the technology, speak to those radical changes that are now upon us, brought about by drones. And when regulators interrogate their own industry, it is important to take note and prepare for such eventualities.

The first of these is the need for the industry to invest more into developing 'sense and avoid' capabilities. Even now, developers are working hard to develop solutions that improve upon the present standard of piloted 'see and avoid', and build drones that are capable of perceiving conflicts to safe flight, such as unexpected weather changes, other aircraft or even birds or simply obstacles within the terrain. The first stage of this process is the capacity to identify and detect the hazard, while the second and third stages are 'separation' from the obstacle, which allows for a piloted deviation from it, to 'collision avoidance', which may involve more emergency procedures to ensure that no contact occurs.

Second, one of the most compelling dimensions of drone technology today is its trend towards greater autonomy, which I have discussed a number of times throughout this book. The 2015 CAA guidelines foreground autonomy as a key aspect of policy development in regulating drones, distinguishing between two kinds of autonomy. These may be simplified as semi-autonomous – 'systems that still require inputs from a human operator ... but which can implement action without further human interaction once the initial input has been provided', they refer to this as 'highly auto-mated'. However, the most controversial category is fully autonomous or 'high authority automated systems', which are those systems that can 'evaluate data, select a course of action and implement that action without the need for input' (p. 64). It is this aspect that describes the realisation of full autonomy, independent of human influence and, perhaps, decision making.

Finally, the CAA guidelines highlight the possibility of 'self-modifying systems', which can learn from the data they acquire and modify their actions, emphasising that present – and likely future – CAA guidelines all presume that:

> *a competent human is able to intervene and take*
> *direct control within a few seconds at any stage,*
> *and that the human will be been [sic.] presented*
> *with enough information to have continuous*
> *situational awareness (CAA, 2015, p.65).*

Yet, this presumption may be in question in future designs. After all, one could quite imagine that the safest course of action in any high risk situation is also best made by a machine than by a human, especially when the human may have actu-ally lost some of their technical know how as a result of the transition from human to machine-controlled systems.

TRUSTING THE MACHINE

One of the reassuring features of drone design is the degree to which, increasingly, they may be described as a closed, intel-ligent system. Set up to make the best decision in any given situation, the drone's decisions are based on the accumulat-ed knowledge of all previous scenarios, which it then seeks to utilise to produce more intelligent resoutions to problems. Indeed, drones or artificially intelligent machines are hardly the beginning of such transfer of knowledge and expertise. Even the mechanical calculator is a step in a direction towards acknowledging the fallibility and limitations of the human mind. It is hardly surprising, then, that we tend more often to attribute credit to a machine's answer, especially in matters of calculation. Moreover, tomorrow's drone will exist in a highly regulated and controlled data cloud, rather than the current wild west of drone operations that we currently see, a hive mind similar to the world wide web.

Yet, ideas about a future world driven by AI are in conflict with broader concerns about humanity's fate and its reliance on the machine in all aspects of our lives. While autonomous vehicles may create safer travel, be more economical and free up people's time, they also raise questions about what is left for people to do, when the machine can do eveything. In a world of autonomous vehicles, people need not worry about the functional problem of having to control a vehicle and can presumably spend their time doing things that are more valuable, important or enjoyable than, say, driving through traffic.

OUR TECHNOLOGICAL CULTURE

This analysis of the gains from autonomous vehicles neglects the fact that function is intimately connected to a range of other social configurations that occur around the function. The twentieth century was defined by the automobile as a vehicle that championed and elevated individual freedom. In this respect, being able to drive one's own car was symbolic of such freedom. The automobile allowed one to occupy a transhumanist space, which was not bound by our biological evolution. Of course, the car was not the first vehicle to do this. Rather, the bicycle and the train are clearly also important innovations along a continuum of technologies that sought to enrich the experience of freedom. However, car driving is unequivocally defining of our times and to suggest this may no longer be available to us meets with some resistance, just because, even if it is likely to be riskier than a self-driving car, people still enjoy driving.

For many people, the freedom to drive a car is intimately associated with the transition from childhood to adulthood, characterising a landmark coming of age moment, of parental and geographic independence. These symbolic associations with human behaviour do not disappear overnight and, even if they are not present in subsequent generations, technology has a tendency to resurface as another cultural form. For example, I was recently in a second hand camera store. In front of me in the queue was a young man of around 17 years old who was inquiring into a whole range of compact manual cameras from the 1980s. These were not the remarkable analogue cameras which only the very serious photographers had access to during the second part of the twentieth century, not Leica, Canon or Nikon. These were the kind of compact cameras that I had growing up, which cost a modest amount of money and which had an electric winder to move the negative forward. These cameras took very average photographs and the high-street developing service rendered them into quite mundane, physical artefacts.

For this 17 year old, these cameras were objects of historic fascination, at the time when mobile, digital photography may be the only camera that people own. He paid nearly nothing for the camera and the shopkeeper explained the mechanism inside the camera, as if it was some magical object when, as I remember it, moving from those cameras to digital – our departure from them was because they were pretty terrible.

In this example, one accesses insight into how devices transition from a situation where they are regarded as high technology – for these were high tech devices in their time, clearly democratising photography – to low technology, but crucially, how low tech may subsequently become more highly valued. In part, this is because that transition becomes imbued with historic meaning. The old camera becomes symbolic of a different time, when we could not just shoot hundreds of photos, as one might with a mobile phone, because there were only 28 negatives available in the camera film.

And so, the history of any technology is not fixed. The drone, as it is currently understood, valued, and used in contemporary society, may yet be redefined again. In this sense, there is no linearity to technological development, no singular manner in which progress may be defined out with a range of cultural conditions. Indeed, it is this kind of realisation that explains why people like to make photographs look old within their Instagram account using vintage filters The loss of degradation that comes from digital content means that we must design the passing of time into the content artificially, as digital degradation consists mostly of either being able to see the image perfectly, or the file becoming corrupt and not being able to see at all. This may also mean that humanity's pursuit of increasingly efficient means through technological innovation has an end point.

Our technological evolution and the singularity described by philosophers and futurologists may be a point at which humanity begins to positively value less efficient means over the most efficient, as it begins to appreciate that such choices would permit greater derivation of value within our lives. This is why it is crucial that our starting point for explaining the cultural, political, economic and social significance of the drone to recognise its function as a prototype, but that it is prototypical not in terms of its function, but in terms of its capacity to transform society.

Drones are a gateway into understanding all kinds of insights into humanity's relationship with technology and our capacity – or not – to adapt to new technological systems. They are ways of prototyping the future, testing out ideas about how else humanity may live. Already, drones have provided insight into what the world may look like when people are surrounded by autonomous vehicles. The tensions they have already created will mirror anxieties that are likely to surround a world where driverless vehicles become a core part of our ability to move around. Indeed, some of the most recent designs speak to a future of drone-based passenger vehicles, flying us around from place to place.

Alternatively, whereas static robots may have been limited in their capacity to replace humans, the drone is not so restricted. In 2011, a fleet of drones were programmed by Raffaelo D'Andrea's lab at ETH Zurich to construct a wall, which signals the beginning of the end of the craft of construction (Guizzo, 2011). This complex, precision-based task, so reliant on the micro-movements and dexterity of human hands, thus, may also be replaced by a drone. Yet, while one may lament the loss of such skills, it is likely that new kinds of skills within construction emerge.

This is why it is so important to consider the drone's impact on the creative act – the artistic project. The naive view of AI is to speak of it as a reduction of creativity when, actually, it is a catalyst for changing the nature of the creative act. Indeed, one can examine the entirety of human history to reveal such developments. From the creation of musical instruments to synthesisers and even photography, technology does not reduce the expression of creativity, it merely adds additional ways through which one may become expressive. Despite photography and animation, people still draw with pencils and do so across their entire lives.

The drone pilot who uses pre-programmed flight paths to capture content may, nevertheless, be able to infuse those paths with content that has creativity and novelty built into it. However, until we see these sensitivities and manipulations of the algorithm develop – until there is a form of creative practice that can get more out of an intelligent system than what is simply programmed – then we cannot know the limit of this trade-off.

There are some major limitations ahead for a drones-based society, not least of which is the question of power – batteries. Despite the move towards electric vehicles, there is a critical environmental impact to battery-based travel systems, which is only beginning to be realised. For drones, one of the key technological challenges is the trade-off between battery weight and power and a lot of investment into better battery solutions preoccupies many developers. For example, in 2014, DJI submitted a patent application for a system that would allow a drone to automatically land in a refuelling station and swap out its battery for another. The patent was awarded in 2016 and gives some insight into how battery limitations may be overcome in the future (Schibanoff, 2018).

A SKY FULL OF DRONES?

A further obstacle to the proliferation of drones is resolving how a fleet of drones would occupy the skies around us. Allocating radio frequency to hobbyist UAV work calls under the role of OFCOM in the UK, and this work is likely to become increasingly difficult. There are also live, global discussions about whether all drones should be registered, much like cars or weapons, with the UK introducing a registration system in 2019. While it is was previously only those in excess of 20 kilograms that required registration in the UK, the growing number of sub-20 kilograms drones is the key issue facing regulators, particularly around the proliferation of small-scale drone solutions.

One compelling consequence of the civilian drone revolution is the way in which it is democratising the occupation of our sky and this is a powerful metaphor to promote social change. Where once flight was restricted to the few, it is now available to everybody – albeit vicariously – through the rise of autonomous drones. Increasingly, one need not have special skills to put flying vehicles into air space, which undertake tasks we set for them. In this respect, drone skyways are commensurate with the broader democratisation of technology that pervade society. From the internet to DNA, there is a global movement whereby the public seeks to take control of the means of manufacturing. One may interpret this shift as a consequence of high technology's aspiration to remove humans from its system to subject them instead to the technological system, which then not only avoid the fallible human tampering, but also traps people into economic transactions.

However, not all will recognise democratising the sky as a step forward in humanity's evolution. It is apparent already that many people find the drone to be an annoyance within civilian space. Indeed, in coverage of some of the first drone delivery systems, people in rural areas – the places likely to benefit most from such means of delivery due to their being limited by connectivity – describe how drones disturb the peace and quiet of their rural environment (Burnside & Roy, 2018). Drones also typically carry on-board cameras, causing some to claim them to be a violation of personal privacy. For, even if one has no reasonable claim to privacy in many social, public spaces, privacy may still be enjoyed and experienced when hiking along a quiet trail, for instance. The proliferation of drones is a threat to the experience of privacy, even if one may argue that no legal claim is jeopardised.

Already, there is evidence of resistance to such circumstances. In 2015, a non-profit company called 'NoFlyZone' was set up, allowing people to register the airspace around their homes as no-fly zones (Athlerton, 2015). The initiative outlined how it would talk with drone developers and ensure that the drones are pre-programmed to respect the no-fly zone guidance. The initiative collapsed after just one year, due to there being no legal force to compel manufacturers to take on such preferences (Drone Business Center, 2016). Yet, its creation highlights the controversy that surrounds ownership of air space and the public's desire to be a part of those discussions. As Rule (2015) describes, where previously there was no pressing need to define ownership of low-level airspace, drones make it a matter of contention that is mostly unresolved legally.

How people feel about such matters in the future remains to be seen. After all, it might transpire that innovation will permit the creation of sufficiently silent drones to avoid annoying people. Indeed, noise reduction has been a key area of research for some years and has an even wider history in aviation with efforts to reduce the sound generated by other flying vehicles (Uragen & Tansel, 2014). Alternatively, people may find ways of resisting the visual capacities of drone using anti-surveillance technology. Indeed, artist Adam Harvey's (2017) 'Hyperface' project developed 'a new kind of camouflage that aims to reduce the confidence score of facial detection and recognition by providing false faces that distract computer vision algorithms'. In this sense, some of the key challenges presented by the proliferation of drones may yet be overcome.

THE ILLUSION OF CONTROL

The twenty-first century drone is yet another manifestation of humanity's desire to exert greater control over its dominion,

a desire which Wall (2012) describes as central to the Enlight-
enment rationality. Yet, the contradictions created by these
ambitions reveal why our pursuit of such power is not wholly
desirable and, in fact, may be entirely illusory. For instance,
if the end point of autonomous drone filmmaking is the erosion of creative filmmaking sensibilities, then, rather than an
enrichment of drone filmmaking, it may create a complete
absence of such intelligence. Imagine a filmmaker simply
choosing their creative style by pressing a button, rather
than developing their own style. Indeed, this is the subject
of concern in Plotnick (2013), which reveals how the expectation of immediate gratification, along with the capacity to
exert power from a distance, has a long history in our design
of interactive systems. Yet, such immediacy may be at the
expense of other ways of thinking about design.

In one sense, the object of technological interfaces is to
simplify the process so well that executing actions could be
described as being as simple as pressing a button – an act
that permits one to assert agency, but which does not require
much effort. Indeed, when Google launched is widely hyped
Glass project, the aspiration of developers was to free users
from the burden of the technological interface. At the time,
mobile devices were becoming vastly intrusive objects, always
imposing themselves upon human interactions. Glass aspired
to change this and, despite its failure in its initial launch, the
designer's aspirations speak to the desire to ensure that a
technology user can perform tasks unfettered by the interface.

However, such efforts to simplify systems or even make
them more intuitive may be to the neglect of the crafting of
experiences and the values that such undertakings involves.
Philosophers may describe such good as intrinsic to the practice itself and that, their loss, is to the wider detriment of the
value experienced by the actor involved in the undertaking.
In other words, if we reduce such activities to simply button

pushing, then we also fail to appreciate its value and, subsequently, impoverish our attribution of value to the activity. Such views are commonplace among technological systems which aspire to simplify or make easier some otherwise complex process and it may run contrary to the logic of technology to choose least efficient means. Consequently, the big decision humanity faces with drones – or any other technology – is over the degree to which it designs the requirement of labour into the interface.

In any case, there is always a period of time when a new technology emerges where society must figure out what it will become and to what uses it may be put. This period may be analogous to the evolutionary process of adaptation. The invention, in itself, does not dictate these parameters. New rules or laws are discussed and then implemented to determine how it fits into our lives. New technological configurations are developed around it, to allow space for the fulfilment of its promise. New user communities emerge who shape its development. New experiences are enjoyed, which subsequently creates new behaviours, expectations and values, as may be said of the new drone racing market. Indeed, humanity is at this point with drones, but it is still a world that is investing heavily into their speculative use.

THE MACHINE IS PRESENT

Whether it is drones for destruction or drones for art, questions arise about the consequences of being able to undertake acts without needing to be physically present in the conduct of certain act. While the discussion about humanity's absence from the field of combat is a powerful context in this discussion, there is a wider point to be made about humanity's use of technologies that elevate our living life through remote interfaces.

Using a drone to undertake graffiti may compromise the activist's status as a radical outsider. The absence of their physical presence for the site in which the graffiti was created undermines its disruptive character. When we know that the person behind the graffiti did not have to locate themselves within the site, this is to the detriment of its potency, as this investment matters in graffiti art. This judgement is not dissimilar from how one might characterise the achievement of reaching a mountain's summit, comparing an unassisted climb with being dropped onto a peak by a helicopter.

There is something important about the graffiti artist's willingness to physically traverse their environment, perhaps even putting themselves in physical danger to reach a space, or just infiltrating zones that have prohibited access. Consider, again, the Banksy mural from Gaza, which creates the illusion of a hole in the wall that divides the West Bank from the Gaza strip. While the premise of the piece would still have meaning and intent were it painted by a drone, the gravitas of the art would be weakened, if the artist – or simply a human – were not present at the time of its being created. We would not attribute the artwork with the commitment it required of the artist who would otherwise need to have put themselves in a situation of risk to complete the work. This is not to say that art always requires the artist's presence, though works like Abramovic's 'The Artist is Present' compels us to consider this importance, at a time when it is increasingly easy to disassociate the artist from the artwork.

Drones are so much more than just amazing technological platforms that allow people to explore the world differently. Rather, they invite us to consider a number of issues that are critically of our time, but particularly about humanity's future use of technology. Drones engage us with conversations about our relationship with machines, how we relate to physical space, how we relate to each other and what kind of world we want to create. There is clear power in the drone's capacity to allow people to occupy space that is otherwise inaccessible. Yet, the option of doing so may also lead people to further remove themselves from the site of human society, just because the machine is suitably equipped to be present on our behalf. In this respect, drones must be situated in a longer technological history which elevates efficiency and ease as an ideology, but which also shows us what kinds of loss we encounter if we continually shape our lives by such aspirations.

The future of drones remains something of a battleground between those who seek to take risks to spark innovation and others who are anxious about the harms that may occur as a result of the transition into a new social configuration. While a media discourse of danger pervades the portrayal of drones, drone developers have also gone to great lengths to show that drones can also save lives. In particular, DJI launched its first consumer grown in just 2013 and has continually highlighted the extraordinary circumstances in which drones have saved lives. In 2018, it released its 'first count of lives saved by drones' (DJI Technology Inc., 2017), which, from media reports, concluded that 59 people had been saved by drones from May 2013 to February 2017, one-third of which consisted of missions involving amateur drone operators. The following year, DJI heralded a historic landmark when finding that 65 people had been saved by drones from May 2017 to April 2018, including 4 people on one day in three separate incidents (DJI Technology Inc., 2018a).

These new acts of human intervention may not yet drown out the other, more troublesome stories of drone applications, but the drone has rapidly gone from being a marginal device to a mainstream application, used as much by real estate agents as it is by explorers. This breadth of use and the efficiencies the drone brings may be the crucial determinant of how much drones are used, but a more restrictive regulatory environment will surely be to the wider detriment of realising such potential.

The analysis of drones from the perspectives of the brilliant, the bad and the beautiful is crucial to appreciating the innovation assemblages that operate around new technologies, where ideas and applications spread across and between sectors, finding new applications in old designs. For example, in 2018, Disney showcased its own graffiti drone, the Paint-Copter (Vempati et al., 2018), not dissimilar from KATSU's radical proposition for graffiti art. However, reporting suggests they plan to use the drone for maintenance work, repairing paint work that may otherwise be difficult to access. Thus, the relationships between innovators, outsiders, radical others and the mundane applications of mainstream uses for technology are not independent of one another. Indeed, many of the design leaders involved in developing the technology work across a number of projects.

While the drone's future seems relatively consolidated worldwide, there remains a great deal of uncertainty over how their eventual proliferation within a range of services will be realised. Presently, designers are working on their own solutions, perfecting delivery or surveillance systems, for example. It is possible that the best solution for a world in which drones perform multiple services is to develop a collective drone resource, which can be accessed by a range of institutions for a variety of reasons. Single drones could be used for any one of these applications and would be capable of servicing any application.

In fact, there is growing evidence of the fact that drone designs will provide a range of functions. For example, in June 2019, Amazon was awarded a patent for a drone surveillance system (Yeturu & Huddleston, 2019), inviting concern that, far from merely being interested in the provision of consumer services, the technologies developed by this gigantic consumer facing company may slip into a range of more controversial applications. In any case, a multipurpose drone network has many appeals, particularly in reducing drone traffic. The alternative is the proliferation of multiple companies making many drone designs and flying them across a predetermined network, rather like how cars operate presently. Whichever one of these futures transpires, it is clear that drones are the first step in a world of autonomous, personalised mobility, and that many other vehicles are likely to follow.

REFERENCES

AAP. (2014). Geraldton businessman whose drone fell from sky, injuring triathlete, mocks crash probe on social media. *The Courier-Mail*, November 7. Retrieved from https://www.couriermail.com.au/news/national/geraldton-businessman-whose-drone-fell-from-sky-injuring-triathlete-mocks-crash-probe-on-social-media/news-story/186bac1f1ec1445bc64e867828c09a25

Airbus. (2019). Airbus' Skyways drone trials world's first shore-to-ship deliveries. *Airbus*, March 15. Retrieved from https://www.airbus.com/newsroom/press-releases/en/2019/03/airbus-skyways-drone-trials-worlds-first-shoretoship-deliveries.html

AirDog. (2014). Kickstarter campaign. Retrieved from https://www.kickstarter.com/projects/airdog/airdog-worlds-first-auto-follow-action-sports-dron

Amazon Prime Air. (2015). Revising the airspace model for the safe integration of small unmanned aircraft systems. Retrieved from https://assets.documentcloud.org/documents/2182311/amazon-revising-the-airspace-model-for-the-safe.pdf

Animal Dynamics. (2019). *Skeeter Sees*. Retrieved from https://www.animal-dynamics.com/skeeter . Accessed on December 7, 2019.

Athlerton, K. D. (2015). Ban drones from your airspace With NoFlyZone. *Popular Science*, February 12. Retrieved from https://www.popsci.com/noflyzone-company-offers-opt-drone-free-skies

AUVSI. (2018). Technology news Oakland University Professor uses UAS to combat ill effects of climate change on crops in Africa. *AUVSI*, March 18. Retrieved from https://www.auvsi.org/industry-news/oakland-university-professor-uses-uas-combat-ill-effects-climate-change-crops-africa

Baker, A. (2017). The American drones saving lives in Rwanda. *TIME*. Retrieved from https://time.com/rwanda-drones-zipline/

Baker, J. (2018). 8 open source drone projects. *Open Source*, February 12. Retrieved from https://opensource.com/article/18/2/drone-projects

BBC. (2015, January 27). Auschwitz: Drone video of Nazi concentration camp. *BBC News*. Retrieved from https://www.youtube.com/watch?v=449ZOWbUkf0. Accessed on October 2, 2019.

BBC. (2019, July 1). Britain's next air disaster? Drones'. *BBC News*.

Beaumont, M. (2014). John Cale and Liam Young review – Cale's drones outshine Young's flying bots in sinister vision of the future. *The Guardian*, September 12. Retrieved from https://www.theguardian.com/music/2014/sep/14/john-cale-liam-young-cale-drone-bot-sinister-future

Belair-Gagnon, V., Owen, T., & Holton, A. E. (2017). Unmanned aerial vehicles and journalistic disruption: Perspectives of early professional adopters. *Digital Journalism*, 5(10), 1226–1239.

Beomshik Kim, Y., inventor; Samsung Display Co, Ltd, assignee. (2018, Feburary 13). US Patent No. 9,891,885.

Bilton, N. (2014). How to take the ultimate drone selfie. *The New York Times*, April 16. Retrieved from https://bits.blogs.nytimes.com/2014/04/16/how-to-take-the-ultimate-drone-selfie/

Bleecker, J. (2009). Design fiction: A short essay on design, science, fact and fiction. *Near Future Laboratory*, 29.

Boucher, B. (2015, May 1). Artist Katsu vandalizes Kendall Jenner's Calvin Klein Billboard with Graffiti Drone. *ArtNet*. Retrieved from https://news.artnet.com/art-world/katsu-vandalizes-kendall-jenner-calvin-klein-drone-293893

Boyle, M. J. (2015). The legal and ethical implications of drone warfare. *The International Journal of Human Rights*, *19*(2), 105–126. doi:10.1080/13642987.2014.991210

Brandt, M. R. (2013). Cyborg agency and individual trauma: What ender's game teaches us about killing in the age of drone warfare. *M/C Journal*, *16*(6).

Bridle, J. (2012, October 11). Under the shadow of the drone. *Book Two*. Retrieved from http://booktwo.org/notebook/drone-shadows/

Bridle, J. (2014, September). Democratic invisibility: Drones & war, Virgin Unite. *Virgin Unite*. Retrieved from https://www.virgin.com/virgin-unite/business-innovation/democratic-invisibility-drones-war

Burnside, N., & Roy, T. (2018, November 10). Whining drones bringing burritos and coffee are bitterly dividing Canberra residents. *ABC Net*. Retrieved from https://www.abc.net.au/news/2018-11-09/noise-from-drone-delivery-service-divides-canberra-residents/10484044

Callaghan, A. L. (2014). Reinventing the drone, reinventing the Navy 1919–1939. *Naval War College Review*, *67*(3),

98–122. Retrieved from https://digital-commons.usnwc.edu/cgi/viewcontent.cgi?article=1295&context=nwc-review

Callaghan, C. T., Brandis, K. J., Lyons, M. B., Ryall, S., & Kingsford, R. T. (2018). A comment on the limitations of UAVS in wildlife research: The example of colonial nesting waterbirds. *Journal of Avian Biology*, *49*(9), e01825.

Cale, J., & Young, L. (2014). LOOP 60Hz: Transmissions from the Drone Orchestra. *YouTube*. Retrieved from https://www.youtube.com/watch?v=y4QQzzU2diM

Carman, A. (2019, June 19). They welcomed a robot into their family, now they're mourning its death: The story of Jibo. The Verge. Retrieved from https://www.theverge.com/2019/6/19/18682780/jibo-death-server-update-social-robot-mourning

Chapman, A. (2014). It's okay to call them drones. *Journal of Unmanned Vehicle Systems*, *2*(02), iii–v.

Charlton, A. (2017, August 17). 'Extremely dangerous' £2,000 dog-walking drone pulled from sale as PR stunt backfires. *IB Times*. Retrieved from https://www.ibtimes.co.uk/extremely-dangerous-2000-dog-walking-drone-pulled-sale-pr-stunt-backfires-1635309

Cirque du Soleil. (2014). SPARKED: A live interaction between humans and quadcopters. *YouTube*. Retrieved from https://www.youtube.com/watch?v=6C8OJsHfmpI. Accessed on October 2, 2019.

Civil Aviation Authority (CAA). (n.d.). Guidance on using unmanned aircraft and drones for commercial work. Retrieved from https://www.caa.co.uk/Commercial-industry/Aircraft/Unmanned-aircraft/Small-drones/Guidance-on-using-unmanned-aircraft-and-drones-for-commercial-work/. Accessed on September 26, 2019.

Civil Aviation Authority (CAA). (2015). *Unmanned aircraft system operations in UK Airspace – Guidance CAP 722* (6ᵗʰ ed.).

Civil Aviation Authority (CAA). (2016). Consumer drone users: An audience insight report. Retrieved from https://dronesafe.uk/wp-content/uploads/2016/11/CAA_Consumer_Drone_Users_report.pdf

Civil Aviation Authority. (2015). Unmanned Aircraft System Operations in UK Airspace – Guidance and Policy CAP 722 7th Edition. Retrieved from https://publicapps.caa.co.uk/docs/33/CAP722_Edition7_A3_SEP2019_20190903.pdf. Accessed on October 2, 2019.

Civil Aviation Authority. (2019, March 7). Air Navigation Order 2016 Publication date: 07 March 2019, General Exemption E 4853. Retrieved from http://publicapps.caa.co.uk/docs/33/ORS4No1294.pdf

Colomina, I., & Molina, P. (2014). Unmanned aerial systems for photogrammetry and remote sensing: A review. *ISPRS Journal of Photogrammetry and Remote Sensing, 92*, 79–97.

Deahl, D. (2017). The failed Lily drone is back as a boring version of itself. *The Verge*. Retrieved from https://www.theverge.com/2017/9/4/16251654/lily-drone-back-mota-group-next-gen

Dent, S. (2019, May 1). A drone delivered an organ to a transplant patient for the first time. *Engadget*. Retrieved from https://www.engadget.com/2019/05/01/drone-delivers-organ-for-first-time/

Department for Transport. (2019). Taking flight: The future of drones in the UK government response: Moving Britain ahead. Retrieved from https://assets.publishing.service.gov.uk/government/uploads/system/uploads/attachment_data/file/771673/future-of-drones-in-uk-consultation-response-web.pdf

Di Benedetto, P. & Colacitti, P., authors; Drone Delivery Canada, applicant. (2019, July 16). United States Patent, No. 10,351239. Retrieved from https://pdfpiw.uspto.gov/.piw? Docid=10351239 &idkey=NONE&homeurl=http%3A%252F%252Fpatft.uspto. gov%252Fnetahtml%252FPTO%252Fpatimg.htm

DJI Technology Inc. (2015). DJI and FLIR systems collaborate to develop aerial thermal-imaging technology. *DJI*. Retrieved from https://www.dji.com/newsroom/news/ dji-and-flir-systems-collaborate-to-develop-aerial-thermal- imaging-technology

DJI Technology Inc. (2017). Lives saved: A study of drones in action. Retrieved from https://www.dropbox.com/s/ q9hl6h4zz4hspku/Lives%20Saved%20FINAL.pdf?dl=0

DJI Technology Inc. (2018a). More lives saved: A year of drone rescues around the world. Retrieved from https:// www.dropbox.com/s/7f6lhzz5mt1fcz0/More%20Lives%20 Saved%202018.pdf?dl=0

DJI Technology Inc. (2018b). DJI refines geofencing to enhance airport safety. *Clarify Restrictions*. Retrieved from https://www.dji.com/newsroom/news/dji-refines-geofencing- to-enhance-airport-safety-clarify-restrictions

Drone Business Center. (2016, May 27). NoFlyZone.org Is No More. *DBC*. Retrieved from https://dronebusiness.center/ noflyzone-is-no-more-10537/

Drone Journalism Code of Ethics. (2017). National Press Photographers Association. Retrieved from https://nppa.org/ sites/default/files/Done%20Code%20of%20Ethics.pdf

Dunne, A., & Raby, F. (2014). Critical Design FAQ, Catalogue for Bunny Smash, Museum of Contemporary Art, Tokyo, Japan. Retrieved from http://dunneandraby.co.uk/ content/bydandr/13/0

Ellul, J. (1964) *The technological society*. New York, NY: Vintage Books.

Entwistle, N., Heritage, G., & Milan, D. (2019). Ecohydraulic modelling of anabranching rivers. *River Research and Applications*, 35(4), 353–364.

Farivar, C. (2016, June 9). Man who built gun drone, flamethrower drone argues FAA can't regulate him. *Ars Technica*. Retrieved from https://arstechnica.com/tech-policy/2016/06/man-who-built-gun-drone-flamethrower-drone-argues-faa-cant-regulate-him/

Fast, O. (2011). 5,000 Feet is the Best [FILM]. Retrieved from http://www.gbagency.fr/en/42/Omer-Fast/#!/5-000-Feet-is-the-Best/site_video_listes/88

Federal Aviation Administration. (2016). Certificate of Waiver or Authorization, Walt Disney Parks and Resorts U.S., Inc., Responsible Person: Manuel J. Regateiro, Waiver Number: 107W-2016-00964, Department of Transportation, US Government. Retrieved from https://www.faa.gov/uas/commercial_operators/part_107_waivers/waivers_issued/media/107W-2016-00964_Disney_CoW.pdf

Federal Aviation Administration. (2019a). Docket No. FAA-2019-0364] – Exception for Limited Recreational – Operations of Unmanned Aircraft, Department of Transportation. *USA Federal Register,* 84(96), 22552–22555. Retrieved from https://www.govinfo.gov/content/pkg/FR-2019-05-17/pdf/2019-10169.pdf

Federal Aviation Administration. (2019b). FAA Aerospace Forecast: Fiscal Years 2019-2039, FAA. Retrieved from https://www.faa.gov/data_research/aviation/aerospace_forecasts/media/FY2019-39_FAA_Aerospace_Forecast.pdf

Fischer, F. (2016). Floating, New York City Drone Film Festival. Retrieved from https://vimeo.com/121674748

Flaherty, J. (2014). The inventors of the Wristwatch Drone share their vision of the future. *Wired*, October 6. Retrieved from https://www.wired.com/2014/10/wear-a-spy-drone-on-your-wrist/

Fleye. (2015). Kickstarter campaign. Retrieved from https://www.kickstarter.com/projects/gofleye/fleye-your-personal-flying-robot?ref=discovery_category_newest&term=drone

Fleye. (2016). Important announcement. *Kickstarter*. Retrieved from https://www.kickstarter.com/projects/gofleye/fleye-your-personal-flying-robot/posts/1682078

FLIR. (2019, April 10). FLIR Completes Strategic Investment in DroneBase. *FLIR*. Retrieved from http://investors.flir.com/news-releases/news-release-details/flir-completes-strategic-investment-dronebase

Fly Nixie. (2014, September 26). Introducing Nixie: The first wearable camera that can fly. Retrieved from https://www.youtube.com/watch?v=kfzqUsGMHE0

Ford, R. (2018). Drone gang 'delivered drugs to prison'. *The Times*, August 31. Retrieved from https://www.thetimes.co.uk/article/drone-gang-delivered-drugs-to-prison-windows-zqvk58h2v

Fortsch, M. (2014, January 31). Microsoft Kinect v2 controlled Parrot AR.Drone 2.0 using Parroteer. *YouTube*. Retrieved from https://www.youtube.com/watch?v=i3Jw3ILR8mQ. Accessed on September 2, 2019.

Gallagher, S. (2013, September 18). German chancellor's drone "attack" shows the threat of weaponized UAVs. *Ars Technica*. Retrieved from https://arstechnica.com/

information-technology/2013/09/german-chancellors-drone-attack-shows-the-threat-of-weaponized-uavs/

Geoghegan, J., Pirotta, V., Harvey, E., Smith, A., Buchmann, J., Ostrowski, M., ... Holmes, E. (2018). Virological sampling of inaccessible wildlife with drones. *Viruses*, *10*(6), 300.

Gertler, J. (2012, January). US unmanned aerial systems. Library of Congress. Washington, DC: Congressional Research Service.

Greenwood, F. (2015). Man who crashed drone on White House Lawn won't be charged. *Slate*, March 18. Retrieved from https://slate.com/technology/2015/03/white-house-lawn-drone-the-man-who-crashed-it-there-won-t-be-charged.html

Gregory, D. (2011). "From a View to a Kill." *Theory, Culture & Society*, *28*(7–8), 188–215. doi:10.1177/0263276411423027

Guizzo, E. (2011). Watch a swarm of flying robots build a 6-meter brick tower. *IEEE Spectrum*, December 2. Retrieved from https://spectrum.ieee.org/automaton/robotics/diy/video-watch-flying-robots-build-a-6-meter-tower

Gupta, A. (2014). Bernal Hill Selfie. Retrieved from https://vimeo.com/91898486

Gynnild, A. (2014). The robot eye witness: Extending visual journalism through drone surveillance. *Digital Journalism*, *2*(3), 334–343.

Haylen, A. (2019). Briefing Paper: Civilian drones, Number CBP 7734, House of Commons Library, British Government. Retrieved from http://researchbriefings.files.parliament.uk/documents/CBP-7734/CBP-7734.pdf

Hammertsin, L., & Niranjan, A. (2018). Rise of drones: African journalists counter lies with tech, DW. Retrieved from https://www.dw.com/en/rise-of-drones-african-journalists-counter-lies-with-tech/a-43511639

Hammond, P. (2013). In defence of drones. *The Guardian*, December 18. Retrieved from https://www.theguardian.com/commentisfree/2013/dec/18/in-defence-of-drones-keep-civilians-troops-safe

Harmon, A. (2003). More than just a game, but how close to reality. *The New York Times*, 3, 1–8.

Harvey, A. (2017). Hyperface. Retrieved from https://ahprojects.com/hyperface/

Hiltner, P. J. (2013). The drones are coming: Use of unmanned aerial vehicles for police surveillance and its fourth amendment implications. *Wake Forest JL & Pol'y*, 3, 397.

Hilton, L. M. (2018). Keeping up with the drones, Berman Fink Van Horn. Retrieved from https://www.bfvlaw.com/wp-content/uploads/2018/03/Keeping-Up-With-The-Drones.pdf

Hodgson, J. C., & Koh, L. P. (2016). Best practice for minimising unmanned aerial vehicle disturbance to wildlife in biological field research. *Current Biology*, 26(10), R404–R405.

Holton, A. E., Lawson, S., & Love, C. (2015). Unmanned aerial vehicles: Opportunities, barriers, and the future of "drone journalism". *Journalism Practice*, 9(5), 634–650.

Hood, G. (2013). Ender's Game [Film].

Hughes, N. (2016, March 2). Drone maker DJI's new Apple partnership inspired by customer crossover. *Apple Insider*. Retrieved from https://appleinsider.com/articles/16/03/02/drone-maker-djis-new-apple-partnership-inspired-by-customer-crossover

Jablonowski, M. (2014). Would you mind my drone taking a picture of us? *Photomeditations Machine*. Retrieved from http://photomediationsmachine.net/2014/09/29/would-you-mind-my-drone-taking-a-picture-of-us/

Jablonowski, M. (2015). Drone it yourself! On the decentring of 'Drone Stories'. *Culture Machine, 16*. Retrieved from https://www.isek.uzh.ch/dam/jcr:ffffffff-a520-2ecb-0000-00005a4dc989/jablonowski_2015_drone_it_yourself.pdf

Jensen, O. B. (2016). New 'Foucauldian Boomerangs': Drones and urban surveillance. *Surveillance & Society, 14*(1), 20–33.

Koebler, J. (2015, March 12). The FAA says you can't post drone videos on YouTube. *Vice*. Retrieved from https://www.vice.com/en_us/article/gvykaq/the-faa-says-you-cant-post-drone-videos-on-youtube. Accessed on September 26, 2019.

Kotz, E. (2012). Bringing the War Home Omer Fast: 5000 Feet is the Best (Sternberg Press, 2012). Retrieved from http://faculty.ucr.edu/~ewkotz/texts/Kotz-2012-Fast.pdf

Lewis, P. (2010). Eye in the sky arrest could land police in the dock. *The Guardian*, February 15. Retrieved from https://www.theguardian.com/uk/2010/feb/15/police-drone-arrest-backfires

Lin, C. A., Shah, K., Mauntel, L. C. C., & Shah, S. A. (2018). Drone delivery of medications: Review of the landscape and legal considerations. *The Bulletin of the American Society of Hospital Pharmacists, 75*(3), 153–158.

Linebaugh, H. (2013). I worked on the US drone program. The public should know what really goes on. *The Guardian*,

December 29. Retrieved from https://www.theguardian.com/commentisfree/2013/dec/29/drones-us-military

Lipinski, D., & Mohseni, K. (2016). Micro/miniature aerial vehicle guidance for hurricane research. *IEEE Systems Journal*, *10*(3), 1263–1270. Retrieved from http://enstrophy.mae.ufl.edu/publications/MyPapers/IEEESys2015-MAVHurricane.pdf

Liverpool Echo. (2010). Merseyside police make UK's first ever flying drone arrest in Litherland. *Liverpool Echo*, February 10. Retrieved from https://www.liverpoolecho.co.uk/news/liverpool-news/merseyside-police-make-uks-first-3430999

Mac, R., & Tilley, A. (2017). How an allegedly fake video killed a much-hyped drone startup. *Forbes*, January 13. Retrieved from https://www.forbes.com/sites/aarontilley/2017/01/13/lawsuit-killed-lily-robotics-drones/#426956fa1557

Marshmallow Laser Feast. (2012). Meet Your Creator.

Martin, J. (2018, January 8). GoPro Karma drone news: now discontinued. *TechAdviser*. Retrieved from https://www.techadvisor.co.uk/new-product/gadget/gopro-karma-drone-news-now-discontinued-3639264/

Mayer, J. (2009). The predator war. *The New Yorker*, *26*, 36–45.

McIntosh, R. R., Holmberg, R., & Dann, P. (2018). Looking without landing—Using remote piloted aircraft to monitor fur seal populations without disturbance. *Frontiers in Marine Science*, *5*, 202.

McNulty, M. (2013). Drone crash lands in Manhattan. *NY Post*, October 3. Retrieved from https://nypost.com/2013/10/03/video-captures-drones-flight-above-manhattan/

Michel, A. H. (2013, October 16). Interview: The Aerial Anarchist, Bard College, Center for the Study of the Drone. Retrieved from https://dronecenter.bard.edu/interview-aerial-anarchist/. Accessed on October 2, 2019.

Michel, A. H. (2017, September). Amazon's Drone Patents, Bard College, Center for the Study of the Drone. Retrieved from https://dronecenter.bard.edu/files/2017/09/CSD-Amazons-Drone-Patents-1.pdf

Miller, J. (2016). Unequal Scenes – Mumbai. Retrieved from https://www.unequalscenes.com/mumbai

Miller, J. (2017). The drone video that sums up global inequality. *The Guardian*, April 25. Retrieved from https://www.theguardian.com/inequality/2017/apr/25/unequal-scenes-drone-video-sums-up-global-inequality

Ministry of Defence. (2016). *Advantage through innovation: The defence innovation initiative*. Ministry of Defence.

Montague, J. (2015). Ending an Albania-Serbia Game and Inciting a Riot, With a Joystick. *The New York Times*, October 7. Retrieved from https://www.nytimes.com/2015/10/08/sports/soccer/as-albania-faces-serbia-meeting-the-drone-pilot-who-ended-their-last-match.html

Mumford, L. (1934/2010). *Technics and civilization*. Chicago, IL: University of Chicago Press.

Murrison, M. (2019, January 8). Has the Mota group quietly shut down? The curse of the Lily Drone Strikes Again. *Drone Life*. Retrieved from https://dronelife.com/2019/01/08/mota-group-quietly-shut-down-lily-drone/

Mystic. (2018). The AI-powered drone that sees and understands. *Kickstarter*. Retrieved from https://

www.kickstarter.com/projects/462720434/mystic-the-most-advanced-ai-powered-drone

National Geographic. (2015). Drones sacrificed for spectacular volcano video. *National Geographic*. Retrieved from https://www.youtube.com/watch?v=zFIWWM0Iv-U

Novak, M. (2019, April 4). This Amazon mothership is terrifying as hell, even if it's completely fake, Gizmodo. Retrieved from https://gizmodo.com/this-amazon-mothership-is-terrifying-as-hell-even-if-i-1833739492

Oakland University. (2018, March 8). Anthropology professor deploys drone to combat hunger in Africa, Oakland University. Retrieved from https://oakland.edu/socan/news/2018/anthropology-professor-deploys-drone-to-combat-hunger-in-africa

Parkinson, H. J. (2014). Is it a phone? Is it a drone? No, it's a flone! *The Guardian*, July 17. Retrieved from https://www.theguardian.com/technology/blog/2014/jul/24/phone-drone-flone

Pavlus, J. (2015, January 15). Something lost in Skype translation. *MIT Technology Review*. Retrieved from https://www.technologyreview.com/s/534101/something-lost-in-skype-translation/

Plotnick, R. (2013). Touch of a button: Long-distance transmission, communication, and control at World's Fairs. *Critical Studies in Media Communication*, *30*(1), 52–68.

Poulsen, K. (2015). Why the government is terrified of hobbyist drones. *Wired*, February 5. Retrieved from https://www.wired.com/2015/02/white-house-drone/

Professional Society for Drone Journalists. (2015). Drone journalism innovator: Drone ban in Kenya hampers social good. Retrieved from http://www.dronejournalism.org/

news/2015/7/drone-journalism-innovator-drone-ban-in-kenya-hampers-social-good

Rattigan, K. M. (2019, June 13). Amazon Prime air's drone design. *The National Law Review*. Retrieved from https://www.natlawreview.com/article/amazon-prime-air-s-drone-design

Regalado, A. (2011, October 31). Who coined 'cloud computing'? *MIT Technology Review*. Retrieved from https://www.technologyreview.com/s/425970/who-coined-cloud-computing/

Rosenthal, E. (2014, May 22). Japanese Dance Company Choreographs performance with Drones. *VICE*. Retrieved from https://www.vice.com/en_uk/article/jpv8qx/daito-manabe-dance-company-eleven-play. Accessed on October 2, 2019.

Savage, C. (2017, March 23). Proposed rules would allow U.S. to track and destroy drones. *New York Times*. Retrieved from https://www.nytimes.com/2017/05/23/us/politics/drone-surveillance-policy.html?_r=0

Reyes, J. (2015, January 9). Penn showed off a smartphone-powered drone at #CES15. *Technically*. Retrieved from https://technical.ly/philly/2015/01/09/grasp-lab-penn-ces15/

Ronald Shaw, I. G., & Akhter, M. (2012). The Unbearable Humanness of Drone Warfare in FATA, Pakistan. *Antipode*, *44*, 1490–1509. doi:10.1111/j.1467-8330.2011.00940.x

Rule, T. A. (2015). Airspace in an age of drones. *Bulletin Review*, *95*, 155.

Russell, J. (2019). Facebook is reportedly testing solar-powered internet drones again – This time with Airbus. *Techcrunch*. Retrieved from https://techcrunch.com/2019/01/21/facebook-airbus-solar-drones-internet-program/

Rwanda Ministry of Health. (2018, May 8). Tony Blair visits Rwanda's drone port. Retrieved from http://www.moh.gov.rw/index.php?id=19&id=19&tx_news_pi1%5Bday%5D=8&tx_news_pi1%5Bmonth%5D=5&tx_news_pi1%5Bnews%5D=1&tx_news_pi1%5Byear%5D=2018&cHash=6e5cb7eefe4a95d267f533a0cb655057

Schibanoff, A. (2018, April 24). Follow the patents: Latest drone technologies give an eagle eye's view of the future. *Electric Light & Power*. Retrieved from https://www.elp.com/Electric-Light-Power-Newsletter/articles/2018/04/follow-the-patents-latest-drone-technologies-give-an-eagle-eye-s-view-of-the-future.html

Schroeder, A. (2014, April 24). Vimeo now hosts a dedicated 'dronie' channel. *The Daily Dot*. Retrieved from https://www.dailydot.com/upstream/dronies-vimeo-channel/

Shaw, I. G. R. (2013). Predator Empire: The Geopolitics of US Drone Warfare. *Geopolitics*, *18*(3), 536–559. doi:10.1080/14650045.2012.749241

Sigufsson, L. (2017). New York's drone superhighway officially launches. *Discover Magazine*, September 29. Retrieved from http://blogs.discovermagazine.com/drone360/2017/09/29/drone-superhighway-new-york/#.W6o-OBMbPOQ

Singer, P. W. (2012). Do drones undermine democracy? *The New York Times*, January 21. Retrieved from https://www.nytimes.com/2012/01/22/opinion/sunday/do-drones-undermine-democracy.html

Sputnik International. (2015, May 8). New Russian Kurganets-25 IFV Uses 'Playstation' Controller. *Sputnik International*. Retrieved from https://sptnkne.ws/dsby

Stelzner, B. (2019). Letter to Lord Nego Hall of Birkenhead. *DJI*. Retrieved from https://terra-1-g.djicdn.com/851d20f7b 9f64838a34cd02351370894/Open-Letter_BBC.pdf

Sterling, B. (2005). *Shaping things*. Cambridge, MA: The MIT Press.

Strawser, B. J. (2010). Moral predators: The duty to employ uninhabited aerial vehicles. *Journal of Military Ethics*, *9*(4), 342–368. doi:10.1080/15027570.2010.536403

Strong, C. R., & Zafra, N. (2016). Natural disaster strategic communication: Drone, data and backpack journalism trends. *PRism*, *13*(1). Retrieved from http://www. prismjournal.org/homepage.html

Swatman, R. (2016, January 6). Intel stuns during CES keynote with record for most drones airborne simultaneously – Watch incredible footage. *Guinness World Records*. Retrieved from http://www.guinnessworldrecords.com/ news/2016/1/intel-stuns-during-ces-keynote-with-record-for-most-drones-airborne-simultaneousl-411677

Taillier, S. (2014, April 8). Triathlete injured as drone filming race falls to ground. *ABC News*. Retrieved from https:// www.abc.net.au/news/2014-04-07/triathlete-injured-as-drone-filming-race-drops-to-ground/5371658

Tatale, O., Anekar, N., Phatak, S., & Sarkale, S. (2018) Quadcopter: Design, construction and testing. *International Journal for Research in Engineering Application & Management*, *4*, 1–7. doi:10.18231/2454-9150. 2018.1386

The People of the State of California v. *Lily Robotics, Inc.* (2017, January 2012). Case Number: CGC-17-446365 Superior Court of the State of California City and County

of San Francisco Unlimited Jurisdiction. Retrieved from
https://regmedia.co.uk/2017/01/13/lily_restraining_order.pdf

Thomas, A. L. R., Taylor, G. K., Srygley R. B., Nudds, R.,
& Bomphrey, R. J. (2004). Dragonfly flight: Free-flight
and tethered flow visualizations reveal a diverse array of
unsteady lift generating mechanisms, controlled primarily
via angle of attack. *Journal of Experimental Biology*, *207*,
4299–4323.

Tucker, P. (2018, May 3). A criminal gang used a drone swarm
to obstruct an FBI Hostage Raid. *Defense One*. Retrieved
from https://www.defenseone.com/technology/2018/05/
criminal-gang-used-drone-swarm-obstruct-fbi-raid/147956/

Turkle, S. (2017). *Alone together: Why we expect more
from technology and less from each other*. New York, NY:
Hachette.

U.S. Department of Transportation. (2018, January 10).
FAA Drone Registry tops one million. Retrieved from
https://www.transportation.gov/briefing-room/faa-drone-
registry-tops-one-million

U.S. Government. (2018, October 5). FAA Reauthorization
Act of 2018. Retrieved from https://www.congress.gov/115/
bills/hr302/BILLS-115hr302enr.pdf

United Nations. (2015). The International Civil Aviation
Organization UAS Toolkit. *United Nations*. Retrieved from
https://www.icao.int/safety/UA/UASToolkit/Pages/Narrative-
Background.aspx

University of Delft. (2014). Ambulance drone. *YouTube*.
Retrieved from https://www.youtube.com/watch?v=
y-rEI4bezWc. Accessed on October 1, 2019.

Uragun, B., & Tansel, I. N. (2014, May). The noise reduction
techniques for unmanned air vehicles. In *2014 IEEE*

International Conference on Unmanned Aircraft Systems (ICUAS) (pp. 800–807).

Vempati, A. S., Kamel, M., Stilinovic, N., Zhang, Q., Reusser, D., Sa, I., ... & Beardsley, P. (2018). Paintcopter: An autonomous UAV for spray painting on three-dimensional surfaces. *IEEE Robotics and Automation Letters, 3*(4), 2862–2869.

Wadi Drone. (2015). Retrieved from http://wadi.io/

Wall, T., & Monahan, T. (2011). Surveillance and violence from afar: The politics of drones and liminal security-scapes. *Theoretical Criminology, 15*(3), 239–254.

Walt Disney Parks and Resorts U.S., Inc. (2015, October 30). Petition for waiver and exemption from FAA Regulations and relief to operate unmanned aircraft systems under Section 333. Retrieved from https://www.faa.gov/uas/commercial_operators/part_107_waivers/waivers_issued/media/107W-2016-00964_Disney_CoW.pdf

Wheaton, B., & Beal, B. (2003). Keeping it real' subcultural media and the discourses of authenticity in alternative sport. *International Review for the Sociology of Sport, 38*(2), 155–176.

Wich, S., & Koh, L.P. (2018). *Conservation drones: Mapping and monitoring biodiversity.* Oxford: Oxford University Press.

Wilke, J. (2019, June 5). A drone program taking flight. *Day One: The Amazon Blog.* Retrieved from https://blog.aboutamazon.com/transportation/a-drone-program-taking-flight

Wing Medium. (2019, April 23). Wing becomes first certified Air Carrier for drones in the US. *Medium.* Retrieved from https://medium.com/wing-aviation/wing-becomes-first-certified-air-carrier-for-drones-in-the-us-43401883f20b

Yang, Y. (2018). DJI seeks new round of financing with company value of $15b. *China Daily*, March 21. Retrieved from http://www.chinadaily.com.cn/a/201803/21/WS5ab1f87da3106e7dcc14426e.html

Yeung, P. (2016). Drone reports to UK police soar 352% in a year amid urgent calls for regulation. *The Independent*, August 6. Retrieved from https://www.independent.co.uk/news/uk/home-news/drones-police-crime-reports-uk-england-safety-surveillance-a7155076.html

Yeturu, K. & Huddleston Jr, H. L., inventors; Amazon Technologies, Inc, assignee. (2019, June 4). Image creation using geo-fence data. US Patent 10,313,638. Retrieved from https://patentimages.storage.googleapis.com/1d/2a/00/3d8d4901aea8e8/US10313638.pdf

Young, L. (Dir.) (2016). In the Robot Skies. Retrieved from https://www.youtube.com/watch?v=cXfYyk0G5Hs. Accessed on October 2, 2019.

INDEX

Activism, 113, 120–124
African SkyCam, 83
AfricanDRONE, 82
Airbus Skyways, 59
AirDog, 31
Amazon, 5, 7, 16–17, 22,
        42, 59
    Patent, 23
    Prime Air, 5, 59
Ambulance, 79–80
Apple, 7, 9, 17–18, 27, 35,
        42, 73
AR. Drone, 32, 80
ArduPilot, 25
Ars Electronica, 129
Artificial intelligence, 60,
        111
Atomics MQ–9 Reaper,
        89
Autonomous vehicles, 69

Babelfish, 114
BBC, 39, 132
Blimp, 60

Chococopter, 28
Choreography, 32,
        116–117, 129, 134

Civil Aviation Authority, 24
    Drone Code, 45
Combat, 89, 103–104, 107
Conservation, 75–79
Consumer Electronics
        Show (CES),
        31–35
Control, 7, 14–15, 17, 27,
        47–51, 57, 63, 68,
        80, 94, 104–107,
        109

Da–Jiang Innovation
        Technology Co
        (DJI), 7
Data, 6, 17–19, 21, 23–24,
        52, 62, 66, 75–78,
        99, 116–117, 119,
        121, 129
Delivery, 5–7, 23, 41–42,
        59, 80
Design, 1, 9, 11–14
DIY Drone, 27, 53
Drone Champions League,
        74
Drone Delivery Canada,
        41
DroneCode, 25

National Geographic,
    75–76
New York City Drone Film
    Festival, 132
Nixie, 33–34, 63
No–fly zones, 40, 44–45, 58

Olympic Games, 116
Omnichen 2, 12
Oneohtrix Point Never, 118
Open source, 25, 27, 127

Paparazzi UAV, 25
Parrot, 7, 17, 22, 24, 32,
    35, 72–73, 80
Patents, 19–25, 60, 81,
    108, 114, 117
Performance, 2, 31, 70,
    116, 118–119,
    128–130
PhoneBloks, 27
Photography, 7, 23, 32, 38,
    67–68, 70, 81, 111,
    123, 131
Pirate Party, 40–41
PlayStation, 94–95, 99
Policing, 58, 89, 108, 110
Predator, 89–90, 110,
    120–121
Presence, 2, 103, 122, 128,
    130, 133
Project Ryptide, 66
Prosumer, 7, 68

Quadcopter, 12, 20,
    33–34, 46, 72–73,
    114–115, 128
Quadrotor, 108, 128

Queen Bee, 1–2

Racing, 20, 31–32, 73–75

Samsung, 23, 81
Selfie, 33, 68–69, 71, 73,
    123–124
Simulation, 94–95, 98–99
Skeeter Dragonfly, 92–93
Snotbot drone, 77
Society of Drone
    Journalists, 85
Spaxels, 127, 129
Sport, 73, 75
Surveillance, 4, 20, 22,
    57, 61, 65, 89, 93,
    107–108, 110
Swarm, 56, 108, 129–130

Theatre, 74, 118, 127
Tree–planting, 66
Triathlon, 49, 51

United Arab Emirates, 66

Wadi Drone, 67
War, 89, 95, 97, 99, 101,
    104, 110, 119, 123,
    132
Weapon, 53–54, 90–91,
    96–97, 105–107,
    110, 119, 122
Wearable drone, 33,
    61, 63
World Drone Convention,
    75

Zipline, 80

DroneSense, 25
Dronie, 71–73, 131

EHANG 1984, 32–33

Facebook, 18, 34–35, 85
Federal Aviation
        Administration
        (FAA), 32, 38,
        42–43, 54, 83, 109,
        117
Film, 3, 5, 8–9, 17, 24,
        31–34, 46, 49,
        52–53, 62, 65,
        68–71, 75–76, 96,
        101, 103, 114, 124,
        128–129, 131–133
Firefighting, 66
Fireworks, 116–117
First person view (FPV),
        14
Fleye, 30, 35, 48
Flir, 25
Flixels, 117
Flone, 25
Follow me' system, 22, 30

Gaming, 75, 80, 96, 98–99
Gatwick airport, 39
Geofence, 40
Google
    Glass, 61
    Street View, 61–63
    Translatotron, 114
    Wing Aviation, 5–6, 49
GoPro, 15, 24, 68
Graffiti, 125–127,
        133–134

GRASP, 16
Gun, 53

Health, 24, 79–81
Higher autonomy, 5, 87,
        123
Hubsan, 24, 57

Intel, 32, 115–116, 129
IRIS+, 47–48

Jibo, 9–10
Journalism, 81–87, 132

Kickstarter, 29–32, 34–35,
        66–67
Kurganets–25, 94–95

Law, 53, 86–87, 107–109,
        124
Leisure, 38, 68–73, 75, 96,
        99
Life–ring, 65–66
Lily Camera, 33, 69
Line of sight, 48, 56, 61

Mars Rover, 12
Marshmallow Laser Feast,
        118, 127
Military, 1, 3–4, 11,
        21–23, 41, 53,
        65, 88–94, 96–99,
        102–104, 106–108,
        110, 113, 120, 130
Music, 2, 118, 128
Mystic, 30–32

NASA, 59